How Can I Help?

How to Support Someone Who Is Grieving

How Can I Help?

How to Support Someone Who Is Grieving

— JUNE CERZA KOLF —

Da Capo

LIFE
LONG

A Member of the Perseus Books Group

Cover Design:	Josh Young
Book Design & Production:	Randy Schultz, Anne Olson
Index:	Michelle B. Graye

Published by
DaCapo Press
DaCapo Press is a member of
the Perseus Books Group
www.dacapopress.com

Library of Congress Cataloging-in-Publication Data
Kolf, June Cerza.
    How can I help? : reaching out to someone who is grieving / June Cerza Kolf.
      p.   cm.
    Includes bibliographical references and index.
    ISBN 1-55561-187-7
    1. Grief. 2. Bereavement—Psychological aspects. 3. Death—Psychological aspects. 4. Loss (Psychology) I. Title.
BF575.G7K635 1999
155.9'37—dc21

                                                       98-51015
                                                             CIP

Contents

Dedication

To my dear friend, Gerrie Meyer, who never needs to ask, "How can I help?" but instead listens to her heart and follows its message. Thank you, Gerrie, for listening to me all these years, for the laughter we have shared, the encouragement you have given me and the tears you understood so well.

Preface

I looked up from reading the obituary column of our local newspaper.

"Oh my goodness, Henry Johnson's wife has died. I'll have to call him right away," I told my husband. His expression clearly indicated he thought I had lost my mind.

"Don't you think you should give him a few days before you call?" he asked me.

Before becoming employed by a hospice organization and working with their bereavement support group, I too would have waited a few days, sent a sympathy card and avoided anyone who was grieving. However, I have learned an entirely new set of rules from spending time with grieving people.

I have learned it is essential to make contact as soon as possible. I have been told the support of others in the first hours of grief is the most valuable gift you can give. Therefore, I knew it was necessary to get in touch with Henry immediately to let him know I was hurting with him. At the same time, I needed to find out how I could help. The only way I could accomplish these tasks was to phone or go to his house. I decided to phone him.

I was surprised when Henry answered the telephone himself. I explained I had just seen the obituary and I was very sorry. In this particular situation, it was Henry who was my friend, not his wife. I had only met her on several brief occasions. Therefore, my concern was for him, rather than the personal loss his wife's death would make in my own life.

Henry sounded genuinely pleased to hear from me. I could hear him catch his breath when I offered my condolences, and he interrupted me in midsentence.

"Craziest thing you ever saw," he told me in his heavy Southern accent. "We were sitting there watching television when Betty said she felt funny, grabbed her chest and fell over."

This was obviously a time when the bereaved person needed to talk about the actual death before he could believe it himself. I encouraged him by asking simple questions without probing beyond anything he wished to offer. I purposely didn't tell him to not think about it. I didn't offer any advice. I just listened with an occasional "uh-huh." I definitely did not interrupt to share a similar story. And I tried not to act shocked or distressed by what he was saying.

Any of those reactions would have given him the unspoken message I could not handle his grief. It would have shut the door that needed to be opened in order to absorb the shock of a sudden death. Each time he told the story, he would be able to grasp the facts a bit more, until at last, he too would accept that his wife was gone.

Henry went into great detail about the way Betty looked. The details were not pleasant to hear, but I had called to help him. Listening was the best way I could do that. When it became obvious he was finished with the details of the death, I steered the conversation toward the plans for the next few days.

People often avoid talking about funeral-home visitations, memorial services or cemeteries. Henry needed to talk about these details before he could face the next three days. He had to verbally walk along the path many times so when he approached the new terrain, he would be able to find his way. I led him with an occasional question, careful not to invade his privacy.

Then I asked about his household situation. Henry told me he had many out-of-town guests. If he had been alone, I would have immediately gone to be with him until his family members arrived. I inquired about the length of time these people would be staying. Did anyone else need to be picked up from the airport? These questions let me know whether help was needed in practical matters. As we talked, I mentally asked myself if I was needed for transportation, extra bedding or a foldout cot. Would a meal be required after the funeral?

I was not merely curious; I was planning my strategy as we talked. It sounded like Henry had everything under control for the moment and that his greatest time of need would be one week later, when his family returned to their own homes.

I hastily jotted down Henry's name on my calendar after I told him I would attend the funeral. Then I told him I hoped to see him after his company left.

"Why don't you pencil me in on your calendar for lunch on March third and I'll talk to you the day before to confirm our plans," I told him. I set a specific date so Henry would have something concrete to look forward to after he was left alone.

The following day, I sent a sympathy card. Although I had not known Henry's wife well, I did have a couple of vivid memories of her. I not only signed my name to the card, I also wrote about these memories on the blank side.

When I attended the funeral, I was generous with hugs for the whole family—even the members I had not met before. As I approached Henry in the receiving line, I hugged him tightly and reminded him of our date for lunch. It was one of the few smiles I saw that day.

"I'll be saving up my appetite just for that," he replied.

At home, I prayed for Henry and his family. A week later, I called Henry to confirm our lunch date. I asked him to tell me honestly if he felt like going out. He said he did. If he had sounded hesitant, I would have suggested taking lunch over to his house instead, or I would have invited him to my house for soup and a sandwich. There are times when the survivor is not up to facing a restaurant because he fears running into people unexpectedly. It is important to be sensitive to the individual needs in each situation.

As soon as we were seated for lunch, I opened the conversation with, "It must be very different to be alone after all these years. How are you getting along so far?" Being specific is better than the general question, "How are you doing?"

We talked much more than we ate. Henry mentioned that he appreciated my phone call and especially my interest in Betty's death.

"Nobody else let me talk about the way Betty died. Every time I started to talk about it, they would pat me and say, 'There, there.' I was so glad you wanted to hear all the details."

To be perfectly honest, I had not wanted to hear all the details, but I knew from working with other bereaved persons how important it is for grievers to be able to repeat the details again and again.

Later that afternoon, Henry mentioned how glad he was to see our date marked on his calendar. It had been a goal for him to aim toward. He said it had been helpful for him not to be faced with a calendar of blank days. It made him realize plans could still be made and life could still go on, even though his wife of 47 years was gone.

During lunch, I brought up the subject of the funeral. I tried to be specific in my remarks. "The funeral was very nice. I really liked the one white rose in Betty's hand. And the minister's message was quite touching."

Henry nodded and began to tell me how difficult it had been to plan a funeral. Few people had affirmed that the funeral had gone smoothly and that it had been a proper farewell to Betty. The death had been such a shock, and Henry worried whether he had made the proper decisions. I reassured him that he had done a superb job, especially under the circumstances.

During our lunch, Henry went over the details of the actual death one more time. The story sounded as if it were a cassette tape being played over and over again. This was a "tape" Henry needed to play. I listened to the story again.

Henry is hard of hearing. I am certain that people at nearby tables who overheard us could not possibly understand the nature of our discussion, but we were in the process of working through grief. Talking about the death plays a great role in the grief process. Grief does not go away if it is ignored or put on a back shelf. Grief needs to be faced, and it takes hard work before a death can be accepted.

In the year since Betty's death, I have heard the story of her death repeatedly. Henry no longer cries when he plays the tape, and he is beginning to shorten it. Soon, I know he will move away from it completely as his acceptance grows.

I also notice that Henry laughs heartily once again and the twinkle has returned to his eyes. When he talks about Betty, it is to recall the happy times and to share the crazy experiences they had as cattle ranchers. At this point, I continue to encourage him to talk about those happy memories.

Henry is quick to hug me and tell me I was a big help to him. It is rewarding to see his progress and to know I played a tiny part in it. While I was helping him, I was learning to be more comfortable with death. Now, when I am faced with losses of my own, I trust I will be able to deal with them more easily.

I was not always comfortable with death. Until I was 40 years old, grief had touched me only mildly. My family had almost seemed exempt. Then, in a short period, five family members and two close friends died. During this same time, I was a co-leader of a bereavement support group and was visiting hospice patients. I was experiencing my own grief as I was reaching out to help others handle theirs. It was a difficult time in my life. As a result of this experience, I realized supportive people play an important role in a griever's recovery and acceptance. The quality of the support a person receives when a loved one dies can help or hinder grief work tremendously.

Although every death is different and each griever is unique, there are many common ways comfort can be offered. ("The Bill of Rights for the Bereaved" on the inside cover lists helpful reminders to keep in mind when offering support to people who are grieving.) In this book, I share the information I obtained during my 12 years as a hospice-volunteer coordinator and grief support-group leader. I hope this information helps you reach out to someone who is grieving.

PART I

The Initial Contact

Responding to the News

W hen people receive the news that someone they know has died, they experience various reactions as their mind works quickly to assimilate the information. They may experience feelings of shock, anger, guilt or a profound, heart-wrenching sadness. As they sort through these mixed feelings, they begin to think about the loved ones who have been left to grieve this loss. They hurt for them. They want to do something— anything—to help ease their pain. Unfortunately, they usually do not know what to do.

Personal Contact

It is of utmost importance to make contact with a griever as soon as possible. Contact in the early hours of grief is one of the most important support factors for grievers. Those who are grieving draw strength and support from others, just as a plant leans toward rays of sunlight for its survival, strength and growth. You need to be there so the bereaved can draw strength from you.

> Contact in the early hours of grief is one of the most important support factors for grievers.

When distance is not a problem, assess the situation and, if it feels appropriate, go at once to the griever. Naturally, there are times when distance makes it physically impossible to do this. In these situations, make a phone call or send a letter without hesitation.

Help from Outside the Family

Each time death has touched my life, I have been surprised at the people who came to offer comfort. They were never the people I had expected. At first, I felt let down and disappointed in those friends and relatives who did not respond at my time of grief. Hindsight has shown me that those particular people would not have been able to cope with my sorrow. The people who came forward were better suited to help. Often, close friends are grieving so intensely themselves that they hesitate to approach the bereaved family. They have nothing left to offer. Instead, people who feel drawn to help step in to support grievers effectively and efficiently. For this reason, you need to listen to your heart to recognize if you are called to offer comfort.

The word comfort comes from two Latin words, "com" and "fortis" meaning, "strengthened by being with." When death arrives, a great need for comfort comes with it. Frequently, close family members are unable to support each other because of their own intense grief. A more distant friend or family member—one who is not right in the heart of the situation—can offer resources, energy and strength that are depleted in the close family. For instance, after parents suffer the devastating loss of a child, they have great difficulty helping each other. Instead of holding each other up, they seem to pull each other down. One social worker compared it to two bent sticks. In a bent, anguished position, no support is possible for anyone.

> The word comfort comes from two Latin words, "com" and "fortis" meaning, "strengthened by being with."

One parent explained that when he was having a good day and was coming up to the surface for air, his spouse was usually fighting to keep from drowning. The frantic clinging pulled the first person back down, which caused resentment, which in turn resulted in anger, guilt and numerous negative feelings. Therefore, do not assume you are not needed simply because plenty of family members are available. Outside help can be extremely valuable to families. Offer it gently.

> Outside help can be extremely valuable to families. Offer it gently.

Caring Touch

Your personal presence cannot be replaced with any amount of floral bouquets, casseroles or sympathy cards. There is warmth— a certain soothing effect—that comes only in the form of human contact. The touch of a warm hand, the hug from strong arms and shared tears are all particularly consoling.

I personally became aware of the importance of physical support from a touching gesture made by one of my nephews on the day of my mother-in-law's funeral. It was a typical frigid November day in Illinois when the thermometer never reached as high as 10F (-40C). My husband and I had dressed in our warmest California clothing—a lightweight coat for me and a business suit for him. The wind was howling across the deserted cemetery and the ground was so frozen that it crunched and crackled under our feet as we stepped out of the car.

Our nephew David helped us out of the car. Instead of walking away, he opened his topcoat, put an arm around each of us and tucked us close to his body. David is a big hulk of a guy and could easily huddle us both inside his overcoat for protection against the wind. We stood that way throughout the graveside service. I never tell this story without getting choked up, my eyes filling with tears. It was not the physical warmth David provided that was most important; it was the shelter of his loving arms and his thoughtfulness that touched us and eased some of our pain. I am thankful for moments and memories of different generations reaching out to each other in times of need.

Helping Is Worthwhile

Karl Menninger has said the central purpose of each individual's life should be to dilute the misery in the world. Every day offers opportunities to do just that—sometimes in large ways, sometimes in small—sometimes by wrapping relatives in overcoats at a cemetery! Instead, people often let inertia, fear or selfishness stop them. Helping a grieving person is one way to dilute the misery in this world. It may upset your plans and throw off your schedule, but the personal rewards you receive when you help others make it worthwhile.

In his book, *A Gift of Hope*, Robert Veninga tells about surviving the losses and the heartbreaks that life sometimes brings. He interviewed more than 100 people to understand how they were able to withstand devastating tragedies in their lives. He made an important discovery about people who survived tragedy. He found they usually remember one person who supported them and offered them hope.

Louise Carroll also writes in "Be a Comfort," *Live* (1987), about a grieving person: "Through his tears he may not see clearly, but his heart will be warmed by the human touch and loving care. Later, he may not remember what was said, but he will remember the warmth and closeness. He will remember there were those who cared. Over his sadness will be a mist of love, and it will help him through his difficult time."

How can we create a "mist of love"? We can create it with sincere concern, a willingness to help, a listening ear, sincere prayers and our physical presence whenever possible.

Chapter 2

Offering Condolences

I t is difficult to know what to say during the first contact with someone who has just suffered the loss of a loved one. Many people avoid the griever because they feel they lack the right words. There are no pat speeches and no perfect words. Instead, they simply need to say what is in their hearts. Antoine de Saint Exupery wrote, "It is only with the heart that one can see rightly; what is essential is invisible to the eye." This is partly because most people are so good at masking their true feelings. Ask a grieving person how they are, and the answer is usually, "Just fine." Probe beyond these stock answers to find out how someone *really* is.

Your Presence Makes a Difference

Sometimes a hug or a squeeze of the hand can express what you are feeling better than words. When I asked grieving people to share with me any messages that had been especially meaningful to them, I was told repeatedly that they could not remember any actual words, but they could list every single person who had stayed near them that first day.

Compassion

Approach those who are grieving with gentle openheartedness or compassion. Compassion means moving beyond sympathy into empathy. It means opening your heart to the bereaved in a soft, gentle way. It means being completely "present" with the bereaved—setting aside your own worries and needs to be completely available for the bereaved.

> Often, being compassionate means not saying anything at all.

Often, being compassionate means not saying anything at all. I witnessed a good example of this when I watched a pastor at the scene of a death. After he had gone to pray with the family by the bedside of the deceased, he came into the living room and took off his jacket and tie. Then, he sat down in a rocking chair and did not say a word.

Our hospice team could tell at a glance that he had settled in to stay and that our job was complete. There was no need for us to linger any longer. The pastor would take care of the bereaved wife until other family members arrived. He brought not words, but compassion with his presence in that home.

Likewise, the night of my uncle's wake, a young man showed up and introduced himself as a student that my uncle had taught in high school 10 years before. The man said my uncle had been a good man and a good teacher. Then he sat in a chair off to the side of the room and remained there the entire four hours. At the end of the evening, he knelt quietly before the casket and then left. I found this indescribably touching, as did other family members. This young man had not needed to speak during those long, dreary hours. His presence spoke louder than words.

> To be able to reach out my hand to someone who is struggling with one of the heaviest loads in life, to make it a tiny bit lighter, gives me a genuine feeling of accomplishment.

Enriching Experiences

I am often asked if it isn't depressing being with someone who has just experienced the death of a loved one. People want to know why I continue to work with those who are dying and their bereaved families even now that I am retired. I tell them my life is greatly enriched by these experiences. To be able to reach out my hand to someone who is struggling with one of the heaviest loads in life, to make it a tiny bit lighter, gives me a genuine feeling of accomplishment.

As a result of my work, my own life has changed. I have become aware of my own mortality. I waste less time over trivial matters. I appreciate every day as never before, and I am continually amazed at how blessed I am. Small, daily inconveniences that used to upset me now seem inconsequential compared to the burdens I see people carrying every single day. So I willingly leave my pleasant life to go where the pain has settled. I know from personal experience how important it is to have the support of others in a time of grief, so I actively look for opportunities to offer that type of comfort to others.

Clichés

When people are uncomfortable or at a loss for words they often refer to clichés. I have learned from speaking with many grievers that the time right after the loss of a loved one is definitely not a time for clichés. Clichés seem too pat, too meaningless and do not help at all. In fact, they make the bereaved person feel even less understood and more alone.

How to Avoid Clichés

Below is a list of the most commonly used clichés, and more helpful statements that express more compassion and caring.

What Not to Say	*What to Say Instead*
Time heals everything.	You must feel as if this pain will never end.
Try to look for the good in this situation.	This is just too painful to bear.
Your loved one is better off.	Your loved one is no longer suffering, but I know you certainly are!
The Lord never gives us more than we can handle.	This must be so very hard for you.

Try not to cry.	It's OK to cry. Cry as much as you need to.
I know just how you feel.	I can't even imagine how you must feel. Just know how much I care.
Everything will be okay.	Please let me help however I can.
Let me know if I can do anything.	I'll call tomorrow to see how I can help.

What to Say

Instead of clichés, grieving people need to hear reassurances that their suffering is genuine and that the life of the deceased stood for something. If words seem to be required, a simple remark such as, "I'm so very sorry," or a specific comment such as, "I'll miss having Jim holler 'good morning' to me when I go out to get my newspaper. He was such a cheerful neighbor!" Or, "Church bazaars will never be the same without Janet. She was always the one with the creative ideas that made those events a success," are better choices than clichés.

Statements that confirm the loss created a void, or simply that the deceased person will be missed, are all appreciated.

Statements that confirm the loss created a void, or simply that the deceased person will be missed, are all appreciated. Short, meaningful memories that can be shared or photographs are also special.

For example, following my dad's memorial service, my parents' neighbor, Gordon, came up to me smiling sheepishly while we were having refreshments. He said, "This may be totally inappropriate, but I have a slide of your mom and dad that I want you to see." He reached into his jacket pocket, pulled out a small slide viewer and handed it to me. Inside was a slide taken of my parents the year before. They were smiling and obviously having a wonderful time. It warmed my heart to see the picture, and I knew it was Gordon's loving way of reminding me of the good times my parents had shared. It also brought to mind a picture of my dad as happy and healthy versus the picture I had of him during his last few days of life.

No, it was not inappropriate at all. It was a beautiful gesture and one I treasure. It put a personal touch on the loss we were all suffering and validated the life that had once been. It is one of the few things I remember about that day. Gordon had lived next door to my parents for 30 years. He was suffering a loss just like our family was, yet he had found a creative, thoughtful way to comfort us. Later, Gordon ordered enlargements of the photograph for all the members of the family and sent them to us.

To help those who are grieving, allow them time to grieve and don't brush off their loss. Your comments can open doors that let in the light of understanding and hope, rather than closing the door with an inappropriate comment. If you stumble, stammer or say something wrong, the survivors realize how awkward you feel. You can simply admit it and say, "Oh, that wasn't what I meant to say to you at all. I just feel so awkward and I hurt so much for you." Honesty is appreciated.

Loss of a Child

When the loss suffered is a child, never say, "Be glad you have other children," or "You're young; you can have more children." Each child is special and no child replaces another. These comments can anger grieving parents and can be devastating. They may also isolate the bereaved even further from society and make them feel as if nobody—anywhere—understands their agony.

Likewise, "Be grateful for the time you had with little Johnny," is not a positive statement. Grieving parents can rarely be grateful for anything. To expect parents to express gratitude at such a time is unrealistic. It can actually cause parents to feel guilty. It is more appropriate to tell the couple you will miss the joy their child brought and that your heart aches for them. There's no need to feel embarrassed if you cry in their presence. It will only reassure them you truly do care.

The loss of a child seems unnatural and people have great difficulty dealing with it. Frank Deford, whose 8-year-old daughter, Alex, died of cystic fibrosis wrote in *Alex: The Life of a Child*, Cystic Fibrosis Foundation (1983), "Old people die with achievements, memories. Children die with opportunities, dreams."

People who have not experienced the death of a child often feel at a complete loss. Those who have been through this agonizing experience are perhaps the best ones to reach out. As a result of their personal heartache, they can truly understand and embrace a newly broken heart. When they have recovered from their loss, they can experience inner peace by drawing on their own tragic experience to support and comfort another with a similar hurt.

I saw a good example of this when members of one of our bereavement support groups were a lovely young couple whose 3-year-old son died suddenly of congenital heart failure. A year later, the mother and a hospital social worker asked me to help them set up a support group for bereaved parents. The group met on a regular basis for several years. The bereaved mother claims it was the healthiest thing she could have done. She felt she could bring about some good from her son's otherwise meaningless death. This young mother is now on a list at the local hospital and is called any time a young child dies in the hospital, day or night. She wants to be notified so she can go to the aid of the parents. When she helps others, her own grief diminishes.

Especially Difficult Circumstances

Young Widows and Widowers

It can be particularly difficult to handle cases of young widows and widowers. These people face a different set of circumstances than others. Often, as early as the funeral, people say, "Well, at least you are still young enough to remarry." As if they could think of remarriage at a time like this! As if they think anyone could ever replace the spouse they have just lost! It is not a helpful or comforting suggestion and hurts the bereaved terribly. Caring friends express concern and reinforce their commitment to the griever. They avoid empty statements or hurtful remarks about remarriage.

Violent Death

Another difficult situation arises when the death is the result of suicide or murder. Survivors are often asked, "Why?"—as if they knew. Violent deaths leave behind unanswered questions. The reason for and details of this type of death are unimportant. Address the devastation, pain and loss instead. Families who lose loved ones to suicide or murder harbor a great deal of pain encased in deep layers of guilt. They need extra tenderness and compassion as they face the days ahead. Let them know you want to help and care, but that you don't need all the details.

AIDS

When a person dies from an AIDS-related illness, their families can feel shunned or as if their privacy has been intruded upon. Often families in this situation feel as if an explanation is needed about the way the disease was contracted. They can feel stigmatized by the death of their loved one at the funeral and in the days that follow.

Support in Difficult Circumstances

To provide support in these particular cases, be open about the loss. Make it clear the tragedy of the loss is more important than the details of how it happened. Let the family know you understand they are experiencing extra pain because of the circumstances. Do not ask for details unless the information is offered willingly. Just be available, nonjudgmental and offer kind, loving support.

> Be available, nonjudgmental and offer kind, loving support.

Listening

As important as what to say is what *not* to say. Be a good listener in the presence of people who are grieving. This is a vitally important skill. Studies show that one of the best ways to work through grief is to talk about it. Grieving people need their friends to listen while they talk away their grief. I have been told the reason I have two ears and one mouth is so I can listen twice as much as I talk. Good advice, but not always easy to follow. Listening skills are discussed in the following chapter.

> Studies show that one of the best ways to work through grief is to talk about it.

Listening Skills

B eing a good listener does not come naturally to most people. It is a learned skill that comes from constant practice. Anyone who wants to work as a caregiver needs to learn active, reflective, effective and sensitive listening skills.

Active Listening

Active listening is a communication technique in which the listener does not interfere with the speaker's message. The listener listens to the speaker without interjecting judgment, advice or analysis. It is a highly effective tool to use to understand what is being said. It is also a useful approach to help others clarify their feelings.

> Anyone who wants to work as a caregiver needs to learn active, reflective, effective and sensitive listening skills.

An active listener encourages the speaker to expand on the problem with statements such as, "Yes, go on," "Tell me more about that," with a nod of your head to show interest.

When the speaker has trouble clarifying his or her thoughts, respond with, "Then this is the problem as you see it," and repeat the information in paraphrases. The speaker then can correct any incorrect assumptions, which will also help him clarify his own thoughts. Active listening keeps the door open for further sharing. It helps individuals express their feelings in words. A listener who shows shock, acts judgmental, condemns or gives advice stifles any further sharing. It is better to show acceptance and support.

Reflective Listening

Reflective listening goes a step further. The listener paraphrases or "reflects" back to the speaker what has just been said. This assures the speaker that he has been heard. For example, the speaker might say, "I'm too tired to even think straight." This is paraphrased back by the listener as, "It sounds to me like you are feeling overwhelmed and exhausted." Another example, "I don't know what to do. There are too many decisions to make," can be paraphrased as, "You must be feeling quite pressured with all this new responsibility."

This is not merely being an echo; rather, it lets the speaker know the listener has heard and understood what was said. It enables the speaker to form his next thought without interruption. It also provides the listener with helpful information to best help the speaker.

Effective Listening

Effective listening involves paying attention to the tone of voice the speaker is using: "I can hear that this situation makes you angry" or "You must be feeling incredibly helpless right now." These statements let the speaker expand on the idea and even find a possible solution for himself, without the listener having to give advice. *Giving advice is generally not helpful to a person who is agonizing over a situation.* A grieving person has so much information to process that receiving advice just adds more confusion to his already stressful situation.

> Giving advice is generally not helpful to a person who is agonizing over a situation.

Sensitive Listening

Sensitive listening is a necessary tool. To listen sensitively means the listener focuses on the *speaker's* thoughts and feelings rather than his own. It involves the listener's full attention and involvement. A sensitive listener uses body language, eye contact, appropriate touching and posture to communicate. The listener sits down instead of remaining standing. He sits close enough to touch the speaker if contact seems necessary. It is better not to sit behind a desk because that places a barrier between the speaker and listener. Sensitive listening means giving the speaker your undivided attention and responding in an appropriate manner that builds trust.

Eye Contact

Eye contact is vitally important. Have you ever been sharing your innermost thoughts with someone who was looking around the room? You probably felt slighted. That behavior sends the message that they are looking for someone or something more interesting than you are.

When you avoid eye contact, fold your arms or lean away from a person, this body language tells the speaker you want to withdraw from the conversation. Instead, express in simple ways that let the person know you have heard what was said.

Body Language

When you listen to grievers, it is important to touch them at the appropriate times. When you hold a hand or put an arm around someone as they try to say something gut-wrenching, you give them courage to express themselves more fully. This allows people to physically feel your support. Likewise, when you ask questions you indicate interest and show you care. To develop a successful exchange of ideas, you often need to be creative in the way you ask questions.

> To develop a successful exchange of ideas, you often need to be creative in the way you ask questions.

Questions Show You Care

There was a person in my life who I felt never cared about me. For many years, I was uncomfortable in her presence. One day, I finally came to the realization that it was because I felt a lack of interest on her part. As I thought about the situation, I realized it was because she never asked me any questions. She never asked, "What have you been doing lately?" or "Do you have any special projects you're doing?" and she never, ever asked about my writing. All these things hurt me and I often wondered why, after so many years, she took no interest in me.

After further thought and consideration, I discovered it was not a lack of concern, interest or caring on her part. Rather, it was the result of a strict upbringing that considered asking questions to be rude or prying. I began to experiment by asking the questions myself. "Would you like to see the dresses I'm sewing for the girls?" I would ask. She always responded enthusiastically. It took a lot of practice on my part before I was comfortable with this, but it brought about an unusually beautiful relationship that never could have developed otherwise.

I once heard someone say, "Questions are like the banks of a river; they channel the flow of the conversation." Asking questions bridges the gaps in conversation. It shows you care. The questions should not be invasive or rude, of course, but show you are truly interested in what matters to the other person.

The purpose of your questions is to introduce a topic—to let the griever know you care and understand the situation. Instead of the generic question, "How are you?" ask a more specific question, "How are you doing living by yourself after all these years?" or "Are you eating and sleeping properly now that you are alone?" There are almost always huge piles of paperwork to be done following a death. You might ask, "Are you making any progress with all the paperwork that is required?" Or in the case of a widower, "Are you handling the household chores all right?" With a widow, ask about car repairs or yard work that was previously handled by her husband. Think about how the loss has affected this particular griever and gently ask questions that show you care.

When the death is the result of AIDS, violence or suicide, asking for details about the death is inappropriate unless the griever mentions it first and shows a need to talk about it. Questions about finances are also taboo unless introduced by the bereaved.

Creative, sensitive listening, interspersed with questions, can be the most helpful approach to offer a person who is grieving. It allows her the opportunity to vent her anger and confusion. It allows her to begin to form plans for the future. It expels the feelings of being alone or abandoned as it comforts, and gives the reassurance that someone does care.

Chapter 5

The Forgotten Griever

U ntil I began working with bereaved people, I never thought about those individuals who are grieving but are not considered the "next of kin." Following a death, the widow or widower naturally gets an abundance of attention. But what about the situation where a grandchild was closer to the deceased than any other family member? This person needs special tender care, but often does not receive it. Assess each situation individually at the time of death. Help to ease the grief of those who are in greatest need—not necessarily only the *nearest* family members.

Chief in Grief

A situation stands out in my mind where a man dearly loved his father-in-law. Dave had never known his own father and his father-in-law had taken him under his wing for more than 20 years. These two people had a closer, more loving relationship than many blood relatives. The real sons in this family had moved out of the area and were not especially close to their own father. At the time of the funeral, the sons sat in the front pew at church. Dave sat off to the side. He was not mentioned during the service when the sons were. At the conclusion, I was surprised to see Dave get up to act as pallbearer. He was considered "just an in-law," when in fact, he was the one hurting the most in the situation.

Whenever a death occurs, think about *all* those who have been affected by the loss and give them your condolences.

Close Friends

Another situation I watched with distress occurred when a neighbor died. Sylvia and Charla were the best of friends. I lived a few doors away and envied their relationship. They shopped together, took care of each other's children, and they seemed to share a special understanding of one another. I wished I had a friend like that! Then, when Sylvia died unexpectedly, Charla was devastated. She pitched right in and took care of the children, made meals for the family and was a regular trouper. I watched with sadness, because nobody seemed to realize the depth of her *own* personal loss. They appreciated all she was doing, but she received little comfort for herself. She was definitely a forgotten griever.

Other Forgotten Grievers

Other frequently forgotten grievers are grandparents, neighbors, fiancés, in-laws and ex-husbands and wives, such as the woman at our support group who had been divorced from her husband, Bill, for three years. She had previously been married to him for 15 years. When Bill died, nobody offered her sympathy and she was not included in the funeral arrangements. She told us Bill's death was an agonizing loss to her. He was a person she had loved and spent 15 years with, and he was the father of her four children. Her children sat in a front pew at the memorial service, yet she had no idea of proper protocol, including where she was supposed to sit, and her place in the service.

> Being remembered eases the loneliness that is left when someone you love passes from your life.

Whenever a death occurs, think about *all* those who have been affected by the loss and give them your condolences. Being remembered eases the loneliness that is left when someone you love passes from your life. It is especially thoughtful to send a note and sympathy card to someone whose best friend has just died. These special people need your encouragement every bit as much as family members.

Chapter 6

Children and Teenagers

O ften, children are the forgotten grievers when a death occurs. At other times, they are given unrealistic expectations to fulfill. I know of one 6-year-old boy who, when his father died many years ago, was told repeatedly, "Now you are the man of the family." How ridiculous! As a result, he felt responsible whenever his mother cried following the funeral, and he certainly did not want to give up his role five years later when his mother remarried. Be especially careful what you say to children.

Children need the opportunity to ask questions and you need to answer these questions honestly. Death is a fact of life. Only when it is hidden does it become terrifying. Allow children to view the body if they so choose. They can touch the body if they are curious. Of course, never force children into situations where they express fear.

Death of a Parent

When a parent dies, many times the child loses *both* parents— one to death and the other to mourning. Include children in conversations after the death and allow them to mourn with the remaining parent. Doing so helps ease the feeling of isolation or abandonment they may be experiencing.

A child's main fear when a parent dies is usually that something will happen to the remaining parent, and then the child will be left alone. This fear needs to be discussed. The remaining

> When a parent dies, many times the child loses *both* parents— one to death and the other to mourning.

parent cannot promise *not* to die, but he can reassure the child that he is in good health and expects to live for many more years. It is important to tell the child about the arrangements that have been made for him or her in the infinitely rare event that the remaining parent does die. The children can be included in these decisions and can be present when the legal papers are drawn. This adds a sense of security to a home torn apart by a death.

Death of a Sibling

When a sibling dies, children fear that they, too, will die. Or, they feel in some way responsible for their sibling's death. They must be reassured that both ideas are not reasonable. They need to be able to discuss their fears and know they will not be laughed at or ignored. They also need to know their life will stay as much the same as possible. The sibling can be talked about and photographs can be displayed, so long as there is balance in the home. The remaining children must not feel neglected or unable to live up to the memory of the deceased sibling.

Death of a Grandparent

A grandparent's death is natural and can be a time of loving reassurances and learning for a child. It is unwise to try to keep the news of a death from a child. Children have a way of knowing what is going on. Openness is the best policy. This is a good time to share our ideas about what happens after death.

A friend told me he had taken his 10-year-old son, Scott, with him when he returned to his family home after the death of his father. Scott had seemed comfortable at the visitation and had not asked any questions. The following day, he sat solemnly through the church service and shook hands like a real gentleman as people greeted him. The family dinner went well, and Scott spent time with some older cousins. However, it was later that night when Scott sobbed in his father's arms that reassured his father that it was the right thing for Scott to participate. "That's the real reason I brought him," he said. "It was so he could cry and experience true feelings."

How Children Understand Death

Children express themselves when they play with friends. When you listen carefully to what they say, you can pick up on their emotions. Any potential problems you detect can be discussed at an appropriate time.

Television has had a great impact on our children. Television can give children mistaken ideas about death. They may not realize that in real life people do not come alive after they have died as they do in cartoons. Also, death is often depicted as violent rather than natural and normal. Discuss these issues and allow children to ask questions and express their opinions and fears about what happens after death.

> Children express themselves when they play with friends. When you listen carefully to what they say, you can pick up on their emotions.

How Children Grieve

Dan Schaefer and Christine Lyons wrote an excellent book called *How Do We Tell the Children*. Dan Schaefer is a funeral director who has observed thousands of children. His book provides straightforward, uncomplicated answers that can help you explain the facts of death to children, from toddlers to teenagers. The book includes a unique Crisis Section for quick reference during the critical period immediately following a death. It makes an excellent gift for any family in which children are among those grieving.

How Young Children Grieve

When children first hear the news of a death, they often act unaffected. Do not misunderstand this reaction. Children process information in small amounts and begin to grieve slowly. One

It is important to get down to their eye level and let children know they have your undivided attention. Be honest, speak meaningfully from the heart.

minute they may be playing normally, then the next minute they might cry uncontrollably. Young children may ask the same questions over and over again as they try to absorb and understand the information.

I once heard a child's grieving pattern compared to a tornado. The tornado touches down, moves up into the sky and then touches down again without any pattern or definite frequency. The cycle is completely unpredictable.

Be honest in your dealings, even with young children, and do not assume they do not realize what is going on. They need your sympathy, encouragement and support, much the same as adults. It is important to get down to their eye level. Let children know they have your undivided attention. Be honest and speak meaningfully from your heart.

How Teenagers Grieve

Teenage grief carries all the same characteristics and needs as adult grief, except it is much more difficult for teens to feel different from their peers. When a death occurs, teens feel conspicuous and think no other teen has ever gone through the same experience. Help can come from books or a support group that reassures the teenager that other young people have indeed had a similar experience.

Most teens are involved in plenty of activities and rides are a welcome offer.

Honesty is important. Stories about their loved one give them extra memories for their mental scrapbooks. They *are* helpful. So are offers to help with practical tasks. "I know your mom is going to be preoccupied the next few weeks, so please don't hesitate to let me know whenever you need a ride somewhere," is a generous offer. Follow up the offer with periodic phone calls to ask about transportation. Most teens are involved in plenty of activities and rides are a welcome offer.

Help in Practical Matters

I n addition to offering support by your physical presence and lending an ear, the grieving family may need help with everyday tasks. When tasks need to be done, like tidying the house, it is better to simply do them rather than ask if it's OK. Unless it requires a major decision, simply go quietly about the job. The phone often rings off the hook after a death. An offer to answer the phone and take messages—or to screen calls—can be a great help, too.

> An offer to answer the phone and take messages can be a great help.

Everyday Tasks

Linens may need to be changed for out-of-town guests and transportation may need to be provided. Clothes for the funeral may need to be pressed or taken to the cleaners. The tasks you can tackle depend on your closeness to the bereaved. Naturally you would not open closets or begin to use the washing machine at the home of a mild acquaintance. Choose what is suitable in each situation.

Food Is Appreciated

If you do not know the family particularly well, but you still wish to help, food is always appreciated. However, keep in mind that the grieving household is generally deluged with desserts and casseroles. It is best to choose something more original, such as homemade soup, cold meats and rolls for quick lunches or a coffeecake for breakfast. Remember to mark any containers that need to be returned with your name and possibly even your phone number. It is easy to forget where the dish came from in the confusion of a disrupted household. Even better, use disposable containers whenever possible.

A friend told me that several hours after her father died, she answered a knock on the door. There stood a neighbor with a large, battered kettle in her hands.

"This is for you," the neighbor said, and quickly left.

My friend lifted the lid and said that her nostrils were greeted with the most delicious aroma. In the pot was thick, rich soup made from chunks of carrots, hunks of tender meat, barley, green beans and even pieces of tomato, all combined in a thick, rich brown broth.

During the next few days, that pot was on the stove almost constantly. It served as dinner the first evening when nobody felt like cooking, but their stomachs were growling nonetheless. It provided a filling, hot midnight snack one night when my friend could not sleep. And she had it bubbling on the stove, making the house smell inviting, when her brother arrived after a late-night flight. The soup was not only nourishing and easy to serve, but it brought with it the feeling of being loved and pampered.

> An easily prepared, simple meal is greatly appreciated.

Another time, I was involved with a grieving family when a friend brought over sliced French rolls, a variety of lunchmeats, sliced cheese and a jar of mayonnaise. She also brought a big jug of iced tea and a package of paper plates, cups and napkins. It made meal preparation simple for the large crowd of people in the house. They were able to fix a meal when they were hungry. Mealtimes can be challenging when people arrive from different time zones. A simple meal that can be prepared quickly is greatly appreciated.

Transportation Assistance

In addition to food, assistance with transportation is often necessary. People who are grieving are easily distracted, but they are not aware of this. Grievers often insist they can drive, light a fire in a fireplace or attempt other tasks that can prove to be dangerous. Watch for these possible dangers and take over the task if it looks like a potential problem.

After my father died, my mother appeared surprisingly capable of functioning. I was surprised by the calm way she made decisions, carried out chores and accomplished tasks. In hindsight, I realize she was in shock and only *looked* capable. Six months later she told me she had no recollection of the days following his death.

The day after Dad died she insisted we needed to go to the bank and I foolishly agreed to drive her there. We were a regular Laurel and Hardy team as I drove in the pelting rain to a place I had never been before.

When she told me to turn, I was already past the parking lot entrance. I tried to go around the block, but all I could find were one-way streets. I managed to get all turned around before finding the bank a second time. We got soaking wet running from the car to the bank and found ourselves laughing in spite of ourselves to relieve the stress.

Inside the bank, the teller was extremely rude as Mom fumbled and dropped her bankbook. Mom gave her the wrong completed form, which was also soaking wet. The teller sighed and spoke to her in a cranky manner. I was tempted to inform the teller that she was dealing with an 80-year-old woman who had not been out of the house for two months and whose husband had just died. Then I remembered to turn my other cheek. I bit my tongue as tears filled my eyes.

Maybe people from the Victorian era had the right idea. They wore mourning clothing to identify those who were grieving. Widowers wore black armbands and widows wore special dresses for two and a half years. They would change the style every six months so that the stage of grief they were in was obvious at a glance. Other specific garb was worn for the loss of a parent, child or other family member and changed at different periods of time.

My experience in the bank that day taught me two lessons: First, grieving people are not as capable at tasks as they appear to be or think they are, and second, you never know what a stranger may be struggling with in their lives.

> Grieving people are not as capable at tasks as they appear to be or think they are.

I want to remember to be gentle in my dealings with others and not add that extra grain of sand to the mountain they may be attempting to climb. Mom and I could have used some smiles that day at the bank, and we certainly would have appreciated it if our errors had been overlooked or patiently corrected. We were functioning at our very best under the circumstances. We could also have used a friend to do the driving for us. We did not think we needed help because we had been grieving throughout my dad's two-year illness, but we were still in a mild state of shock. That is the reason it is so important for people to be on hand for the grieving, merely waiting and willing to assist.

Different Responses

W hen approaching a bereaved person, be aware that circumstances of the death can make a difference in their ability to function or cope. When a loved one dies after a long extended illness, the family has had time to adjust to the idea of death. On the other hand, when people experience a sudden, unexpected death they often suffer from shock. These people often need immense assistance, tenderness and consideration. They find it hard to function, and they move around as if they are in a thick fog. This is a time to tread cautiously and not cause additional pain. (See chapter 9 for more on shock.)

Anticipatory Grief

When a family has been caring for a terminally ill loved one for any length of time, they are partially prepared for the death. These families usually started their grief work before the death, which is called *anticipatory grief.* Funeral plans have often been discussed and decisions may have already been made. There is some shock to deal with, but certainly not the devastating shock that comes when a death occurs suddenly and unexpectedly. The coping and functioning levels in these situations are quite different.

> When a family has been caring for a terminally ill loved one for any length of time, they are partially prepared for the death.

Extended Illness

My family experienced anticipatory grief prior to my father's death. He lived for two years after he was diagnosed with cancer. He responded well to treatment, which resulted in many months of quality time as we all prepared for the inevitable. Dad spent many hours each day making lists and organizing his affairs for my mother. He talked about death, leaving no loose ends. He also spent time reaffirming his love for his family.

When his death finally came, gently and quietly, we were saddened, but also relieved. We had watched his life lose all its quality and we had watched him gracefully tolerate the many indignities imposed on the terminally ill. It was time for him to move on. We knew we would miss him, but we also knew we would be reunited someday.

In our minds, we had imagined the moment of my father's impending death many times. When the actual time came, we were ready to face it. My mother insisted on calling friends and relatives personally. After that task was completed, my mom and I went outside. Mom had been indoors for several months, so she welcomed this bright, sunny April afternoon. We discovered the first perky yellow daffodils of spring just peeking out of the soil and we rejoiced in the warm sunshine on our faces. Neighbors saw us in the yard and came over with kind words and hugs.

Acceptance

Everyone was prepared for this death, and acceptance had begun months before. Our reactions and the stages of grief we experienced were relatively mild. Friends, neighbors and relatives did not hesitate to approach us. We appreciated seeing and hearing from people. Within hours, the house was filled with people and it remained that way until after the funeral.

Our reactions to my father's death were quite different from what they would have been with a sudden, shocking or brutal death. Under those circumstances, people are more hesitant to go to the survivors because they are in shock themselves and are unsure of what to say or do. The months of anticipatory grief protected us from the shock that is experienced with sudden deaths.

The Shock
Factor

S hock is what nature provides to allow people to carry on
under unbelievable circumstances. It cushions, protects and
allows for survival when it would be impossible to function
otherwise. Shock wears off slowly as the body
begins to adjust to traumatic news, and helps
ease a person gently toward recovery. Shock
is a *natural* protector. It is not recommended
to mask it with drugs or for friends to try to
ease it away. It serves an important purpose.

> Shock is a natural protector. It is not recommended to mask it with drugs, or for friends to try to ease it away.

As mentioned in the last chapter, the
shock factor is not as common when death
follows a lengthy illness. Sudden deaths,
however, spark a shock condition that can last for months. People
affected by it often stare into space, distracted and consumed by
grief. People in shock do not need to be pressured into making
decisions. They need the quiet strength offered from hugs, pats
and kind words.

Physical Symptoms of Shock

When an unexpected death touched my own life, I noticed I
experienced a wide variety of physical symptoms that I did not
experience after my loved ones died following lengthy illnesses.
I had problems with dizziness, shortness of breath, nausea,

diarrhea, insomnia and nightmares. These are all normal signs of shock and grief, so I waited for them to disappear naturally.

Occasionally a doctor may need to assess a griever's severe symptoms and treat the condition medically. However, no one should depend on drugs to mask or avoid grief's acute pain. Drugs are best used to treat a specific symptom as a temporary measure only. If the bereaved person seems too agitated to sleep, for example, a mild medication may be prescribed for a few days. Rest is essential at such a stressful time. Even in a controlled situation, be careful with medication; it's easy for a griever to become dependant on it. It may be just as helpful to remind the griever these unpleasant physical symptoms are normal for someone who is grieving and that they are likely to go away on their own eventually.

> In addition to forgiveness, practice endless patience.

Behavioral Symptoms of Shock

Unless absolutely necessary, do not ask questions or expect immediate decisions from the bereaved. Talking seems to bother grievers during the period of extreme shock. Try not to engage the bereaved person in lengthy conversations. Instead, allow her to sit quietly with her thoughts as she sorts out her situation.

During the initial shock, grievers often feel fragmented. They often cannot remember names or details. They are easily distracted. Their memory seems to be nonfunctional. They are often irritable or even verbally abusive to their loved ones, who must understand the cause behind the abuse. Forgiveness needs to flow freely during this time period. It is important not to pressure the griever during this terribly stressful period.

> Try not to engage the bereaved person in lengthy conversations. Instead, allow her to sit quietly with her thoughts as she sorts out her situation.

Decisions are extremely difficult to make under such stress. Delay major decisions if possible. Making funeral arrangements is a heavy burden for anyone to handle. Gently advise when necessary and act as protector if anyone else is applying too much pressure for decisions.

In addition to forgiveness, practice endless patience. Grieving people often ask the same questions over and over and forget the answers. They need to be gently reminded of details. They cannot be held responsible for anything they say during this time. They may react defensively, and it may seem like nothing meets their approval. These are all normal signs of shock and grief.

Closure

I mmediately after a death occurs, or while survivors are participating in the rituals of the funeral, they need unconditional support. The speed and quality of the griever's acceptance and recovery depends greatly on the closure that takes place between loved ones and the deceased. Never stand in the way of proper closure because you feel uncomfortable or are concerned about what others might think. Support the griever by allowing him to choose the best way to gain closure.

Never stand in the way of proper closure because you feel uncomfortable or are concerned about what others might think.

Unconditional Support

A good example of this took place after my uncle died. The death came as a tremendous shock to me. I had no opportunity to prepare for his death or to say good-bye to him. However, all of the arrangements had gone smoothly until it came time for us to leave the cemetery.

We had formed a procession following the casket up a long, steep path to the gravesite. After the military ceremony was completed, we all walked back downhill to our cars. As we approached our car, I hesitated and turned to my husband, Jack. "I just can't leave like this," I told him. He could have replied, "Oh, come on, just get in the car," or, "The ceremony is over and we have to leave now." But he didn't. Instead, he thoughtfully asked, "What do you want to do?"

I was not sure exactly what I wanted to do. I just knew I needed to go back up that hill. The wind was blowing and it was bitter cold, but when I asked if we could return to the grave, my husband took my hand and nodded. We did not worry about the other mourners or the weather as we hiked back up the hill. The cemetery workers were ready to do their job, but they backed away as they saw us return. I did not worry about them either. I put both my hands on the casket and had a private conversation with my precious Uncle Joe. After I said my final good-bye, I motioned to Jack, who was standing a short distance away waiting patiently.

My husband held me close as I said one last prayer before starting down the hill a second time. Now I was able to breathe deeply and the heaviness that had surrounded me earlier had disappeared. Those few moments alone at the casket had given me the private closure that no other part of the formal rituals had provided. If my husband had not supported me in this need, I would have gotten in the car and left the cemetery with agony still enveloping me. My grief would have had to slowly work its way beyond that point before moving on, instead of being released in a quick, more natural manner.

That episode helped me to understand the logic behind the experts' claims that losses need closure. Statistics show deaths that take place as a result of war or accidents are the most difficult for people to accept. They believe this is due to the lack of closure—not seeing the body, not being allowed to grieve normally. Saying good-bye in a way that is comfortable to each individual is important. Be cautious not to take this away. Instead, support grievers by encouraging them do what they feel is necessary.

> Statistics show deaths that take place as a result of war or accidents are the most difficult for people to accept. Experts believe this is due to the lack of closure—not seeing the body, not being allowed to grieve normally.

Steps toward Closure

At one of our support group meetings, a widow shared that she was planning to have her husband's favorite, beat-up cowboy boots bronzed to use as a doorstop. To me, this sounded like a unique and clever way to keep something special of his around the house.

After the meeting was over, one of the other group members did not get up to leave. After some sighing and throat-clearing, she told me she thought the idea of bronzing the cowboy boots was morbid and unhealthy. "You must do something to prevent her from doing this," she begged me. I sat down and explained that each of us finds comfort in different ways. *As long as the task or activity is not harmful to the griever or to anyone else, it is perfectly all right.* Allow grievers to decide what will serve as their solace.

Likewise, when my mother died, I had what some may have felt were unusual requests. There were only two items I wanted from my mother's home following her death. One was her wedding dress. Her mother had made the dress entirely by hand, and I had tried it on frequently in my childhood. The other was an old, rusty watering can. I am a tole painter and I had great plans for that watering can.

> It is important not to discount what gives the griever pleasure.

My siblings were happy to get rid of the watering can and nobody had any interest in the wedding dress, so I was fortunate. I have since painted the watering can and it sits in a place of honor in my home. It is important not to discount what gives the griever pleasure and solace. You facilitate grief work when you offer your support and help grievers who want to fulfill even seemingly strange or unusual actions or ideas.

PART 2

The Week after the Funeral

The Importance of Support

A week after the funeral, the support that originally sustained the survivors usually decreases. Out-of-town guests have to return home to fulfill their own responsibilities. Friends and neighbors stop bringing food. Special attention is withdrawn. This is when those who have taken a backseat need to come forward.

Offer Specific Support

Your concern, presence and help can make a difference in the progress the bereaved person will make. "Let me know if I can do anything," is an empty offer. Be more specific. "How about coming over for dinner on Sunday night?" is a far better approach.

Share a Meal

Mealtimes can be extremely difficult, and a date for any meal is a welcome change. Having breakfast with a friend starts the day off right and gives the griever an incentive to get out of bed, get dressed and leave the house. Instead of automatically going to a restaurant, invite the griever to your home for a meal shared with your family. It can be most welcome, especially if you have children. Children lighten up a situation and can offer a brief respite from the hard work of grieving.

> Mealtimes can be extremely difficult, and a date for any meal is a welcome change.

Meaningful Gestures

Another thoughtful gesture is to send flowers to the home of the bereaved with a note that says he or she is in your thoughts and heart. One widow told us about a bouquet she received a week after her husband's funeral. It consisted of tiny pink rosebuds and dainty baby's breath, all placed in a delicate glass vase with a lace edge. It made her feel pampered and loved every time she looked at it. It reminded her that she was important at a time when she felt insignificant, insecure and alone.

This is a good time to get out your calendar and mark the six-month anniversary and one-year anniversary of the death. Both dates are important times to make contact and offer support. The bereaved person usually has these dates firmly implanted in his memory banks and it means a lot to him to know someone else remembers and cares. A telephone call or a card is sufficient—but a visit or lunch date is even better.

When an Adult Loses a Parent

When adult children experience the death of a parent who does not live nearby, support is frequently lacking. This happens often in today's transient society and with military families. The phone rings in the middle of the night with the tragic news that a parent has died. The adult children leave town to attend the funeral and are gone for about a week. When they arrive back home after this sorrowful trip, the death seems unreal. The deceased parent was not part of their everyday life, yet a great loss has taken place.

> A support group can take the place of extended family, and can fill a real need.

In these cases, extended family support is not available, and there is usually no one to discuss the loss with or to support the grieving person. A support group can take the place of extended family, and can fill a real need.

Thoughtful Gestures

When my father died, he lived halfway across the country. I was fortunate to spend the last month of his life helping to care for him and was with him at the time of his death. Five days after his death, I was back in California, where the entire past month seemed unreal to me.

Waiting for me when I arrived home was a large, red clay pot of spring flowers left by my friend Diane. I felt a surge of unexpected joy as I looked at the pansies with their little velvet faces. While I was out of town, I had missed the special, short, desert springtime, but now I had these lovely little flowers to make up for it. They made me feel as if I had been missed and that my grief was shared. These were the only flowers I received, and I cherished them.

A similar thoughtful gesture occurred when my mother was in her final illness. I spent a month with her and felt like a displaced person so far away from my husband and children. Imagine my surprise when I went to her mailbox one day and found a letter addressed to me mixed in with my mother's mail. A friend had called my husband to get the address so she could drop me a note to cheer me up. And cheer me up it did!

Adjusting to a New Way of Life

Grieving people whose loss drastically changes their way of life, as in the case of a child or spouse, usually have a much more difficult adjustment than when an adult child loses a parent. Under those circumstances, life doesn't just resume, as mine did. Nothing is the same again. It takes considerable time for the bereaved person to adjust. To provide help with this adjustment, listen to what the bereaved thinks are the problem areas.

The griever may begin to express concerns for necessary changes. "How will I ever manage financially?" she may ask. Never respond lightly to such fears with a platitude, such as, "The Lord will provide." Reflective listening can be an effective response to questions like these. "It sounds like you are especially concerned about your finances," would be a suitable response. (See chapter 4 for further explanation of reflective listening.) As the grieving person talks about his or her problems, it becomes easier to sort out the possible solutions.

Offers to help balance a checkbook, straighten out paperwork or find phone numbers for the Social Security office are all practical ways to help. The bereaved person needs to know that this problem, or any other one, does not have to be faced alone.

Fear of Abandonment

Psychologists have found that the number-one fear of human beings is the fear of abandonment. When you stand nearby with your physical and emotional support, this fear is lessened for the griever.

As in the time of the initial contact, the mere presence of another human being is important. It relieves the fear of abandonment, just a little bit. A single white rose waiting on a colleague's desk when she returns to work after a death, or a short note that lets the griever know she is in our thoughts are examples of extra-special ways to say, "You are not alone."

In addition to thoughtful little gifts, this is the time to walk on tiptoes around the griever. It is not the time for locker-room pep talks. Being overly cheerful around a person whose heart is heavy is as bad as stealing his jacket in cold weather or rubbing salt into his wounds. The griever feels supported when you temper your mood to his.

> Grieving people need to be given time to grieve. Rushing them back into a flurry of activity only prolongs or delays grief.

Grieving people need to be given time to grieve. Rushing them back into a flurry of activity only prolongs or delays grief. Just as you would not pull a man out of bed and make him run up and down the hospital halls the day after a severe heart attack, neither should you force a grieving person in his convalescence. Broken hearts of every sort take time to mend.

The death of a loved one is a wrenching, shocking blow to the body. Like a heart attack, it requires time to heal properly. The recovery time of each person is different and you must adjust yourself to his or her schedule.

Support Systems

A person's previous support system makes a big difference in his grief process. A person who assesses his support systems before his life is touched with the loss of a loved one finds he has more support. It is important to branch out and make changes when a person finds that his or her entire support is held in the hands of one person. Suppose 90% of a person's support comes from his or her spouse. If that spouse were to die, the loss would leave him not only without his loved one, but also without any significant support system.

> A person's previous support system makes a big difference in his grief process.

I became aware of the importance of personal support systems while I was working with two completely opposite families who were grieving. Claudine and her husband Tom had been retired for many years. They traveled in their recreational vehicle and spent most of their time together. When Tom was diagnosed with lung cancer, the friends they made while camping came to their aid. They listened as Claudine poured out her fears and helped her when she cried. As Tom became sicker, they took turns helping with his care and even stayed overnight so Claudine could get more sleep.

When Tom died, these special friends stood by her during the following months when she was grieving. I noticed that although she missed Tom, she was able to carry on in his absence and was soon taking out the recreational vehicle on her own. The year that Tom was ill allowed Claudine to build a strong support system for the days ahead.

On the other hand, when Sylvia's husband Jim died suddenly of a massive coronary, she looked around and realized that Jim had become her only friend in the years since his retirement. They spent almost every waking hour together and little by little their outside support system had vanished. Sylvia had no warning and no time to develop the support she would need during her grief. The months ahead were even more difficult because of the lack of support.

When you evaluate a griever's support system, you more fully understand the course of his or her grief work and are able to help him or her. If no support system is in place, you may be required to do more. Never judge or compare people's grief. Instead, try to be understanding and come to their aid in areas where no other support is available. Tread lightly when offering help and offer assistance so you do not add any extra stress.

Appropriate Support

One woman told me that her birthday occurred a week after her husband's death. Her three children had planned a surprise party to cheer her up. At the party, they got out the old home movies, thinking it would be great fun. The woman did not consider it fun to sit and look at the happy times she had shared with her spouse. To her, they were like knives thrust into her heart. When she had stood all she could, she left the room in tears, much to her children's distress.

It is natural and normal for grievers to be despondent and it is not your responsibility to cheer them up. Rather, acknowledge their sorrow and allow it to progress at its own pace.

It was too soon for her to take part in this activity. If she had been consulted, she could have chosen a more appropriate way for her family to celebrate her birthday—a way that she could have handled at that time. It is natural and normal for grievers to be despondent and it is not your responsibility to cheer them up. Rather, acknowledge their sorrow and allow it to progress at its own pace.

Delayed Grief

A member of our bereavement support group, Bob, told us that the day after his wife's funeral, his daughter needed to return to her home in a distant state. She insisted that Bob go with her. He ended up staying several weeks and then went to visit other relatives who insisted he stop by. *Rushing the bereaved into frantic activities too soon is almost always a mistake.*

Bob came to our group almost a year after his wife's death and realized he had not grieved previously. One of the biggest disadvantages to delayed grief is that very little support is offered after a time lapse. The bereaved person is expected to be "over it" by then. He or she is not encouraged to talk about the loss and does not receive any other assistance.

Research has uncovered that one of the best ways to recover from grief is to talk about it. On the bulletin board over my desk is a calling card from an organization that provides grief support. It states, "Every Loss Needs 100 Tellings." I put it there to remind myself to listen. When I received that card, I thought back to my own losses and roughly totaled the times I was able to "tell my story." I came up with an average of six times for each loss. It made me aware that there are remarkably few people encouraging the necessary talk about the experience of death.

Meaningful Gestures

I n the early weeks following a loss, you may want to offer more original tokens of support than you did at the time immediately following the death.

A Personal Touch

A simple way to do this is with a card that says you are thinking about the person who is grieving and his family. Be sure to add a note, photograph or some personal touch. A card without a letter or note is not particularly meaningful. It only takes a few extra minutes to write a sentence or two and it means so much more as the family rereads these messages.

> A personal touch is truly meaningful at a time like this. It shows a deliberate caring and thoughtfulness, rather than the impersonality of following the standard procedure.

Poetry also seems to be especially helpful at a time of loss, and members of our bereavement support group often shared poems they had received enclosed in sympathy cards. I have seen families who have kept a box or basket filled with these special items and who were still rereading them years later for comfort. Rarely have I seen a card kept and treasured that had no personal note in it.

Donations

If no particular place has been designated for donations, there might be an organization that has special significance to the bereaved family. Did the deceased work with children? How about a donation to sponsor a child at camp. Did she love to visit the forest? How about having a tree planted in her name in a national forest. Was the death the result of cancer or heart disease? A donation to a related research organization might be appropriate. Do the grievers include children? Often trust funds are set up for the children in the family. If they have not been, you might want to help organize one.

Thoughtful Gifts

A personal touch is truly meaningful at a time like this. It shows a deliberate caring and thoughtfulness, rather than the impersonality of following the standard procedure. My daughter, Kathy, shared an unusual, inventive and thoughtful way she reached out to a neighbor whose mother had died.

A couple of weeks after the funeral, Kathy noticed that her neighbor's lawn needed to be cut. Normally, the teenage boys in the family took good care of the grass, but under the circumstances, apparently it had been forgotten. Kathy hired her gardener to cut their grass for a month and then notified the family that she had lined this up. Kathy said they were most appreciative of her unusual gift, especially the boys. At this particular time, having the grass cut filled a bigger need than flowers or casseroles.

Remembering the Funeral

Your attendance at visitations and funerals shows you care. When you attend these events, it is not for the deceased, but rather for the remaining loved ones. It is not necessary to have ever known the deceased. This is a time of coming together and participating in a formal ritual of grieving. It is a time that the remaining loved ones have chosen to acknowledge the closure of a life that has come to an end. Whether you agree with the methods chosen to express this closure is unimportant. You are not supporting the rituals or the system; you are supporting the grieving people who are left behind.

Your first contact with the bereaved following a funeral should include some mention of the event. Funerals are often planned in such a hurry that afterwards the loved ones are left to wonder if they made proper choices. You can reassure them and mention specific personal touches that you found meaningful or special. Grievers usually like to have the opportunity to talk about the funeral and they need to know you are comfortable with this.

> Your first contact with the bereaved following a funeral should include some mention of the event.

Help Grievers Take Time for Themselves

With a little forethought, even teenagers are able to reach out and help a griever. After I returned from Illinois to my home following my mother-in-law's funeral, I was quite distraught. I couldn't seem to settle down and accomplish even simple daily tasks. I'm sure it was obvious to my family that I was in a constant state of agitation.

My daughter, Laurie, although only a teenager at the time, was always "tuned in" to any distress in our family and she apparently gave my situation considerable thought before coming up with a plan of action.

When Saturday morning arrived, she said, "Hey, Mom, want to go out to the abbey today?" I wasn't able to do much else, so I agreed. To get to the nearby abbey, we had to drive about an hour on mostly deserted country roads. The sign outside the gate of the abbey clearly states, "No Hunting, Except for Peace."

We parked our car and walked the Stations of the Cross. Then we walked around the pond and watched the ducks float by. The air was still and quiet except for chirping birds and other sounds of nature. I could feel myself unwinding. I looked down the hill and saw a monk, dressed in a hooded robe, belt and sandals, approach the large cast-iron bell. The sound of the bell echoed across the pond. Following the clangs of the bell, we heard the monks chanting the noontime mass.

We are not Catholic, but it didn't make any difference. The tranquil atmosphere soothed us and I felt ready to join the world again. It was the best activity Laurie could have planned, and I was grateful to have such a thoughtful daughter.

Employers and Employees

A griever usually returns to work after one week. I am told that frequently co-workers ignore the fact that a death has occurred. Nobody mentions it at all; it is as if nothing has happened. I believe this is because people are afraid they will remind the griever of the death and make him or her uncomfortable if they mention it. However, the death is the main thing on a griever's mind and no one else has to mention it for the person to remember. Not mentioning the death only makes the grieving person feel isolated and abandoned.

> Not mentioning the death only makes the grieving person feel isolated and abandoned.

Acknowledge the Loss

If the loss has been that of an elderly parent, a simple "I'm sorry to hear about your dad," can be adequate to acknowledge the loss. Even this short statement can reassure a grieving person. A pat on the back, a hug or an offer to help them catch up on their work all go a long way.

If the bereaved person acts as if he or she wants to pursue the conversation by beginning to talk about the deceased person or about details of the funeral, this is the time to stop, sit down and practice active listening. (See chapter 4 for further explanation of active listening.)

If the loss was more significant, such as that of a wife or child, then it is necessary to be even more understanding. Such persons may remain in shock, even after they have felt it was necessary to return to work. They may not realize the disoriented, easily distracted condition they are in. They may want to return to work to put some semblance of order back in their lives, even before they are completely ready.

Work Assignments

If possible, lighten the bereaved person's workload or assign them tasks that are easily accomplished and not critical to the company. Certainly, mention the loss and give the griever freedom to discuss it whenever possible. Acknowledge that a painful loss in their personal life has occurred. Ask how you can help, both on and off the job.

Safety

In some jobs, workers must maintain peak performance for their own safety and the safety of others. Employers must acknowledge it could take several weeks or even months for a grieving employee to regain that level of performance.

A small amount of extra time and caring may help the progress of the grief process.

Often, the more concentration a job takes and the more involved the person can become, the easier it is to forget the loss temporarily and do their job well. But if the job becomes too much to handle, find the griever an alternative, temporary position in the company. Provide the reassurance that as soon as she is ready, she can move back into her former job.

Extra Time and Caring

Each person's situation differs and each must be carefully evaluated. A little extra time and caring may help along the grief process and actually minimize the time and efficiency lost by valuable employees. Grievers need to know they are secure in their jobs at a time when they face so much disruption elsewhere in their lives.

People who work side by side have interesting relationships. When I stopped working, I missed the daily contact with the same people. I had often spent more time with them than with my own family. They were a wonderful support system for me when I suffered losses or experienced joy. Because of their close proximity, co-workers and bosses can offer a unique support system to grievers, with little effort.

Sharing Memories

In addition to listening to stories about the deceased, now is the time to share memories. People need and like to have mental scrapbooks that they can use to recall special memories. You can help put these mental scrapbooks together by sharing stories, letters or photographs as soon as the survivor is able to appreciate them. You can do this whether you have just met the griever or are a life-long friend.

A Common Loss

I noticed at my uncle's funeral that almost everyone explained who they were when they introduced themselves to me. "I'm Jayne. I went to school with your cousin," or, "I'm Bill, the next-door neighbor who owns the horses." Although I had not met them previously, I could connect their stories to similar descriptions I had been hearing for years from my uncle. It made me feel as if I were with old familiar friends.

These were the loving, caring people who filled my uncle's life when I was unable to be with him. These were the people with whom I now shared a bond because of our common loss. It was reassuring to know I was not the only one facing a void in my life. The ache I felt was *shared*.

Photographs, Letters and Stories

If you have a photograph you feel the family may not already have and might like a copy of, it is a generous gesture to send them one. If you live a long distance away and are unable to visit, a letter that tells about an experience you shared with their loved one may give them great pleasure.

When my mother's next-door neighbor Gordon died, I wrote a long letter to his wife sharing some of my fond memories of her husband. I told her how 35 years earlier I thought I might never get married because Gordon always seemed to be walking his dog when my boyfriends were saying goodnight to me. Gordon, a sociable sort, would stop and visit with us and the dog would jump all over my dates.

Ruth wrote back that she had forgotten about that and it gave her quite a laugh. She added that maybe Gordon was just screening my dates and waiting until he felt the right one had come along. If so, he made a good choice. My marriage has lasted over 30 years!

Even little comments that show the deceased person is missed are meaningful.

A call when there is a rare desert snowfall to let your friend know you remember how much her husband loved snow can mean a lot. Or a note following a function where the absence of the deceased was especially obvious lets the griever know you also miss his or her loved one. All these are little ways to share in a loss and bring consolation to a griever.

People who are grieving tell me that the most hurtful thing people do is fail to mention their loved ones. "It is as if my special person never existed and I am the only one who misses him," they tell me repeatedly.

Special Days

Remembering a birthday or anniversary after a person has died is always a thoughtful way to let grievers know they are not the only one who knows today would have been a special day. After our fathers died, both my husband and I remembered our parents' anniversaries, not with an anniversary card or gift, but with a card to the surviving spouse to let our mothers know we were thinking of them on that day. "I'm glad you married such a nice man," I wrote to my mother, "so I could have him for a father. I really

This is a time to be creative. What special memory can you share to ease the pain or loneliness of a recent griever?

miss him!" She telephoned when she received my card, and we had a nice long-distance talk sharing how we missed my dad and remembering some special times.

Decision Making

A week after the funeral it may be necessary to make certain decisions. Major decisions can still be postponed, but insurance papers may need to be filed, bank accounts straightened out or names deleted from legal documents. Bills continue to arrive and financial matters cannot be left unattended.

Household Arrangements

When my neighbor's young wife died, it was all he could do to return to his job and try to make arrangements for his children. His first major concern was to find a housekeeper so he could return to work. The neighbors gathered together and helped him find someone suitable. However, we did not realize we stopped too soon with our help.

After Bill returned to work, his phone was shut off. Next, his trash was not picked up and finally the water was turned off. We were afraid the housekeeper would quit! Apparently, all these bills went unnoticed while his wife was in the

> Each decision the griever makes is a step on the road to recovery. Offer praise and encouragement for each of these small steps.

hospital and remained that way after her death. It caused him unnecessary stress and expense to have the utility services reconnected. Had I realized, I could have reminded Bill about these items and even offered to go through the piled-up mail with him to help decide what mail needed immediate responses and what did not.

Organization

A simple task, like sorting through mail, seems monstrous on top of grief work. Offer assistance to diminish the task. Driving to the bank and standing in line with the bereaved person can ease the strain. Organizing a list of items that need to be taken care of in order of priority might also be helpful.

Support Decision Making

Listening as grievers weigh the pros and cons on matters helps them reach their own decisions. As they talk, and you listen, the situation becomes clearer in their minds and it is easier for the grievers to make decisions. Talking them through often solves problems. Each decision the griever makes is a step on the road to recovery. A caring friend can offer praise and encouragement for each of these small steps.

> Listening as grievers weigh the pros and cons on matters helps them reach their own decisions.

The Grief Process

G rief can begin the first time a widow sees an envelope addressed to "Mr. and Mrs." and realizes the "Mr." is no longer living. Or it might begin the first time a grieving mother is asked by a new acquaintance, "How many children do you have?" and she doesn't know how to answer.

Grief can begin as a person goes to pick up the phone to call his or her dad to share a bit of exciting news, and realizes he is no longer there to answer the phone when it rings. Grief can be finding a tiny pink stocking in the laundry basket after a person's baby daughter died from sudden infant death syndrome. Grief shows up unexpectedly, with a jolt—like an electric shock.

Offer Hope

The type of friend a grieving person needs during his or her grief process is one who does not give advice, but who stands patiently nearby, watching, popping up when necessary and pitching in with practical assistance. A friend can provide an ear, a hug or reassurance that the bereaved person can survive this awful ache. True friends are those who listen not only with their ears, but with their hearts. They listen to the same stories and complaints over and over, offering hope when life seems hopeless.

In the beginning, survivors know they have suffered the loss of a loved one, but they have not yet adjusted to life without them. Adjusting to a new life takes time and hard work. It is helpful when a friend stands close by acting as a crutch.

The Symptoms of Grief

The most common symptoms of grief seem to be shock and denial, crying, anger, guilt, depression and finally, acceptance. These symptoms do not occur in any certain order or last any specified amount of time. A person may pass through each stage quickly or get hung up in one stage for a long time. The stages may repeat without any pattern, and not every griever experiences every symptom.

Denial and Shock

The first symptom people usually experience with grief is denial. "Oh no, it can't be true," are often the first words spoken upon hearing devastating news. However, this stage quickly passes into shock, which is similar to a state of numbness. Shock acts like a natural protection allowing people to survive agonizing news or situations. It's referred to as "nature's Novocain." While in shock, people may walk around in a daze and act differently than normal.

A week after the funeral, some shock still is present. The survivor breaks through the surface of his ocean of grief, looks over the situation, and either continues to tread water, or begins to swim toward shore. A thick fog still surrounds him so he cannot see the shore clearly yet.

Let the Griever Lead

At this time, let the bereaved person set the pace. Let him suggest the tasks he wishes to do. It is perfectly all right if nothing is done. The grieving person may choose to wear clothing of the deceased, sit in the deceased's favorite chair or eat only the deceased's favorite foods. If it brings comfort, it is not unhealthy or morbid.

I have heard some unusual stories of events that took place during this initial period of shock. It's best not to judge these actions, and instead, try to understand the reason for their occurrences. As outsiders, allow grievers the freedom to work through this loss in their own personal way, as long as it doesn't cause any real harm to themselves or anyone else. As the shock wears off, these seemingly strange acts usually disappear automatically. Sometimes these actions distress other family members, but that needs to be dealt with separately.

> Grievers need tremendous support and comfort while they are in shock, much as people recovering from anesthesia after surgery need to be tended to gently and carefully.

Shock usually wears off gradually as grief's deep wound begins to heal. Grievers need tremendous support and comfort while they are in shock, much as people recovering from anesthesia after surgery need to be tended to gently and carefully.

In a rare situation, there is no shock immediately following a death. Such was the case with Vivian, who called me the day after her husband's funeral. She wanted to join our bereavement support group and wanted some additional information. Usually, we advised people to wait about six weeks before joining. The pain is too fresh in the beginning for the wound to be touched. After six weeks, enough healing has begun that help can be given. I explained this theory to Vivian, but she insisted she was ready to attend the very next day.

It turned out that Vivian was one of those unique people who thrives on facts. She seemed to experience no shock or numbness at all. The more she knew about grief, the quicker she felt she would recover. She dug into every book on our suggested reading list, and quizzed us extensively. She went and spoke to the coroner, the paramedics and every person who had been present when her husband collapsed from a massive coronary. She carefully studied all the details and within two months was reaching out to help others who were grieving.

Every person grieves differently and helpful friends set no limits.

It would have been a mistake to slow her down. *Every person grieves differently and helpful friends set no limits.* They just walk beside the griever at whatever pace he or she chooses to set.

Personal Belongings

Allow the griever to clear out or remove the belongings of the deceased. Unless the bereaved person requests it specifically, it is a mistake to think it is helpful to remove these articles yourself. A good portion of grief work takes place from handling these items. Removing clothing and personal items yourself denies the bereaved the opportunity to experience the grief they are entitled to feel. Tears that are shed while these tasks are performed are cleansing and healing. They come from deep inside and wash away deep-seated hurts.

A young woman who suffered a stillbirth shared that while she was in the hospital her sister had gone to her home and packed away all the baby items. Her husband had also taken down the crib and bassinet and packed them away in the garage. When she walked into the house with her empty arms she was greeted with an empty room that had once been a nursery. She said her heart broke a second time.

She had been thinking about that special room she had lovingly prepared. She was planning to sit in the rocker and nurse her broken heart. She knew she needed time to slowly change gears and holding the tiny baby items would have been good therapy.

However, it is perfectly permissible to offer assistance in the tasks that would be too difficult to be done alone. I have stood by many a closet while the bereaved person took out articles of clothing and handed them to me. I folded each item and placed it carefully into a box.

We have done this quietly, side by side, sometimes laughing over a faded, worn-out article of clothing that should have been thrown out years before and sometimes crying as we handled the favorite items that were almost like the deceased's uniform.

Transferring each item from the closet to the box, we were removing the deceased person a tiny bit from our lives—gently, slowly, carefully and quietly.

Crying

With a sudden death, shock and all the frantic activity surrounding the funeral can sometimes delay crying. Some people cry more after the first week as the death becomes more real to them. Most people feel uncomfortable when someone cries in their presence and are not sure how to respond.

> Some people cry more after the first week as the death becomes more real to them.

Putting your arms around a person or holding a hand, and allowing him to cry is often all that is necessary. This may occasionally feel awkward to you, but it does not feel awkward to the recipient. If the bereaved person isn't allowed the freedom to cry, he or she doesn't receive that necessary comfort.

I have the bad habit of going into the privacy of the bathroom to cry. I sob silently into a bath towel, soaking it with my tears. Then I dry my eyes, wash my face and attack life once more. This may release my immediate stress, but it certainly does not provide the loving care my family could give me if I allowed them to see my tears.

When people are constantly given the feeling that it is too uncomfortable for others when they cry, they resort to hiding in the bathroom. Give grievers permission to cry. It's good to be able to cry and it's perfectly all right to let others see our tears.

Science has proven that tears release deep emotions that words cannot. They cleanse and soothe an aching heart. "Crying is one of the healthiest things you can do," writes Bob Deits in *Life After Loss*. "Studies have shown that tears of sadness have a different chemical makeup than tears of joy. Tears of sadness release substances that have a calming effect. It is no myth that you feel better after a good cry." Any broken-hearted griever can use tears to soften his or her heart. Allow grievers this privilege.

At our bereavement support group meetings the very first thing we did was put a box of tissue in the center of the table. We jokingly referred to it as "Our Attractive Centerpiece." We told our members that it was perfectly acceptable to cry in our presence. When people began to cry, we never tried to stop them. Usually, it created a chain reaction and everyone joined in. Sharing tears with a group helps the griever feel less isolated and lonely.

Anger

Flashes of anger may begin at any time in the grief process, but usually escalate at some point. Anger is probably the most difficult stage to deal with, both in ourselves and in others. Many people are taught early in life that nice people do not get angry. They spend years learning to be nice even when they don't feel especially nice.

Death makes us angry. We are angry that our plans for the future have been disrupted. We are angry at God for the dirty deal he gave us. We are angry at others who have not lost a spouse, child or loved one. We are angry at the doctors, the mortician, the weatherman, the bank teller. In fact, we are angry at everybody and everything. Unfortunately, when this sudden anger is shown by grievers, nobody knows what to do with it.

Anger Can Be an Expression of Fear

Experts have discovered that anger is very often a response to fear or pain. The death of a loved one causes the bereaved to feel tremendous amounts of both these emotions. Consequently, the anger grievers express may actually be the expression of an underlying fear or painful emotion. Sometimes simply encouraging and allowing grievers to talk about their fears helps diffuse the anger.

> Anger is often a response to fear or pain.

When dealing with grievers, it is important to acknowledge that anger is natural and normal as long as it doesn't harm anyone. Do not try to talk them out of it by saying, "The doctor did his best," or "God must have his reasons." It is better merely to listen, and sometimes ask creative questions that help channel the anger along a nondestructive path. Expressing anger in this manner gradually removes some of the pain and fear they are experiencing.

Anger can be frightening to watch. People usually do not know what to do when a person seems out of control. I once watched a woman shake her fist and scream out her anger in front of our group. It scared me. However, the therapist who was leading the discussion just sat and listened until the woman was finished. Then she told her we could all feel her anger, and that it was justifiable because she had suffered a terrible loss.

The therapist let her know we understood and cared, and then went on to suggest constructive ways to get rid of the anger. One suggestion was to have an imaginary conversation in private with the person who was the main focus of her anger. Most important, the anger was not rejected or treated as anything except normal.

Helping Grievers Vent Their Anger

Therapists have an appropriate term they use in regard to anger. It is called *venting.* I like this word because I can picture a teakettle with the spout as the vent. When the water begins to boil, the steam is vented out of the spout, much the way people can vent their anger when it reaches a "boiling point." With a teakettle, you can raise the flame or lower it to control the amount of steam that is vented.

People who are grieving can be encouraged to treat their anger in the same way. The best way to let them know they can do this is to allow them to continue once they begin. Sensitive listeners allow anger to vent rather than shutting it off. Shutting off the steam can cause internal pressures to build and explode at a later date.

> *Face underlying issues.* In addition to being a good listener, it often helps someone vent his or her anger if you have him or her stop and think about the underlying reason for the present anger. What is causing the most pain? What is he or she most fearful about? Often just identifying the cause and labeling it makes the anger vaporize.

Engage in physical activity. Another excellent way to vent anger is through physical activity. Suggest attending an exercise class together or going on a daily morning walk. A good fast game of tennis, a bike ride or other stimulating activity done with a friend can work miracles. You can be that friend by suggesting the activity and participating in it with the bereaved person.

Write and journal. As a caregiver, you might suggest that writing has proven to be an important tool in working out anger. No one has to see the written pages; they simply serve as a therapeutic means to rid the mind of harmful thoughts.

Ruth said that she began journaling shortly after her husband died. In the beginning, she wrote so fast and furiously that her pen went right through the paper. As the months passed, her writing became less frantic and erratic. As she reads back over her journal, she can see the way she progressed. She says she went from black days to gray ones to pure white ones in a two-year time period.

Dan thought he had a better solution than writing to vent his anger. He broke an entire set of dishes one Saturday morning. He said he had never liked the dishes and it felt oh-so-good as each one crashed to the floor. Not something I would have suggested, but if it works . . .

Guilt

Guilt begins to slink around as soon as the fog of shock lifts. Any statement that begins with, "Why didn't I?," "I should have," or, "If only," is destructive. Discussion about regrets helps dissipate guilty feelings. The more often feelings are verbalized, the clearer each regret becomes until it can be mentally resolved. Being a good listener is the best antidote.

Guilt can eat away at people and bring on severe physical symptoms. Energy is wasted where it does no good. Instead, this energy could be directed toward acceptance and the adjustment to a new way of life. Do not discount the griever's guilt by saying, "You have no reason to feel guilty." People cannot help the way they feel. Instead, let them know you understand their feelings, that guilt is normal during grief work and that you are there to help them face these feelings and work through them.

Helpful Exercises

Families in which the death was the result of a murder or suicide are often consumed with guilt. Suggest daily journaling as a release of guilty feelings or even simple list-making. (See the box below for an example exercise.)

Exercise to Process Guilt

Start with three columns. Write down the guilty feeling in one column, whether it is justified or not in the next column and then a solution in the last column. If there is no solution, it can be left blank until a solution seems possible. For example, in the case of a suicide:

Is the guilt realistic?	Can the situation be changed?	Is action necessary?
Suicide was not the griever's choice.	The past cannot be undone.	Educate the griever about suicide.

For instance, when Dawn's fiancé committed suicide, she felt it was her fault. "I should have realized the depth of his depression," she kept repeating. Her feelings were real but they were not justified. To help her gain peace over the situation I used the above exercise.

Is the guilt realistic? "Could you have prevented the suicide if Cliff was determined to end his life?" I asked Dawn whenever she expressed her guilt. I told her suicide is a private and personal decision made when life becomes unbearable. It can be delayed but the final act is the suicidal person's choice.

Can the situation be changed? The past cannot be undone. However, past experiences offer valuable lessons. I suggested to Dawn that she should put her pain to use by reaching out to other suicide survivors. She joined a support group, shared articles she had found helpful and offered compassion to others in the group as her own wound began to heal.

Is action necessary? In Dawn's situation there was no action, such as an apology, to ease her guilt. She read copious material relating to suicide, kept a daily journal and attended a support group. All these tasks helped her gradually move beyond her guilty feelings and closer to accepting her loss.

When you ask non-intrusive questions and suggest the griever write down his feelings, it serves to steer him onto the path where he can begin to set his guilty feelings aside. Tread gently with these people. Do not ignore their guilty feelings. Remember: Feelings are always valid, whether or not the guilt is. This is the time to put your listening skills to work and allow the griever to vent.

There are numerous excellent books pertaining to grief. (See the appendix for a list of books.) This might be the time to present one as a gift. It helps the bereaved person better understand the stages they are experiencing and offers solutions to the common problems faced by grievers. It helps them realize their experiences are natural and normal, and all part of the grief process.

Depression

Depression is the most common and long-lasting part of the grief process. It is also the most debilitating, because it comes wearing many different disguises. It can appear as insomnia, loss of appetite, lethargy, extreme fatigue or a complete disinterest in life. When helping someone who is depressed be extremely sensitive to the signals you receive from that person.

A good way to ease depression is through conversation. If grievers are allowed to verbalize their feelings, depression can often be lessened. To help those who are grieving, encourage them to talk about their feelings and their concerns.

> A good way to ease depression is through conversation. If grievers are allowed to verbalize their feelings, depression can often be lessened.

New Interests

Developing new interests can be constructive. A week after the funeral is too early for this, but tentative plans can be made. This gives the bereaved person something to look forward to without putting stress on him or her to begin the activity too soon. Suggesting a griever enroll for a full class schedule at a local college would be unwise, but offering to take a single class with her in a few months would be an excellent idea.

Physical Activity

Another way to ease depression is with physical activity. Offer to accompany the griever on an activity, such as a walk on the beach, a hike in the serenity of the mountains or a quiet drive in the country.

Medication

Do not recommend grievers use antidepressant drugs unless they have a history of clinical depression. These medications rely on chemical action. It can take time to build up to the proper dosage. Therefore, it is not an especially effective means of relieving normal grief symptoms in a non-clinically depressed person. People need to be allowed to experience all aspects of their grief to work out their feelings and reach a point of acceptance. When true feelings are masked with medication, it delays normal, natural feelings, which can result in delayed grief reactions.

Alcohol is another form of self-treatment that grievers sometimes use. "A glass of wine will relax me so I can sleep better," is a common fallacy. Alcohol is considered a stimulant and might actually have a reverse reaction. Any substance can become habit-forming to a griever who is already in a weakened, vulnerable state of mind.

A glass of warm milk or a cup of hot decaffeinated tea are better choices. A wide variety of herbal teas are available that are specifically formulated to naturally calm, soothe and relax people. Soothing music during a quiet time prior to bed can aid in relaxation. As a caregiver, steer the griever away from stimulating television shows or telephone conversations right before bedtime. It is helpful to wind down before going to bed.

> A wide variety of herbal teas are available that are specifically formulated to naturally calm, soothe and relax people.

Acceptance

Acceptance may not be reached for many months, or possibly even years. It is the final stage of grief, the one grievers have to work toward.

To move forward, grievers have to reach the point at which they can say, "I do not like what has happened. I do not like living without my loved one, but I have no choice. I have to pick up the pieces and make the best of life from now on." This happens slowly, with gradual adjustments and reorganization.

> Acceptance begins after the fog lifts and the griever begins to find new ways to add joy and pleasure to life.

Acceptance begins after the fog lifts and the griever begins to find new ways to add joy and pleasure to life. Even after acceptance has been reached, there still are moments of sadness and tears. However, the griever no longer feels as if he is drowning in his tears.

As acceptance is reached, the isolated "good moments" appear more and more often. At last, they are the most prevalent times in each day. How long does it take the bereaved to reach the point of full acceptance? The answer is, however long that particular person needs. As caregivers, remember that there are no specific rules or time tables. Each griever must proceed at a speed that is comfortable to him or her. You can only walk alongside the griever, allowing him or her to set the pace until you arrive at your destination.

Physical Problems

For a grieving person, physical symptoms usually begin about one week after the death. The distractions of guests are removed, the numbness is beginning to wear off, and shortness of breath, chest pains or other symptoms are more noticeable. If you hear a bereaved person express concern over any physical symptom, suggest he or she see a doctor. As a friend, offer to drive him or her to the doctor and sit with him or her in the reception room.

> If you hear a bereaved person express concern over any physical symptom, suggest he or she see a doctor.

Depressed Immune System

There is always a chance that the symptoms are the result of a genuine ailment. Be careful not to ignore symptoms indefinitely with the assumption that they are part of the normal grief process. When the body's systems slow down due to grief, illness is able to take a greater hold. Colds can last for months, and stomach disorders seem to occur daily. It feels as if every germ the bereaved person is exposed to turns into a major illness.

Grievers may neglect themselves for months while caring for their loved one who had a lengthy illness. A visit to the dentist or the purchase of new eyeglasses may be necessary to help restore physical well-being. Sometimes a grieving person has delayed a necessary surgery. Because the healing process may be slowed in grievers, this is a time for second and possibly third opinions before rushing into the hospital. Also, alert the doctor to the mental condition of the griever before surgery. Grievers need extra support from family and friends during these times.

Anxiety

Anxiety attacks and feelings of great fear may appear at this time. The bereaved person may be living alone for the first time in his or her life, and this can be terribly stressful. In addition, there may be deep-seated fears of financial problems. Offer to help find assistance to overcome these fears, and reassure the person that you will not abandon him or her. A person with a broken spirit needs a crutch just as much as a person with a broken leg. You may have to act as that crutch until the person is completely mended and able to stand alone.

PART 3

The First Six Months

Offering Support

I n the early weeks following a death, grieving people are treated as if they are special. They receive extra attention and consideration. Unfortunately, this special treatment decreases about the same time they need it most. After the fog and numbness that surrounds them lifts, the void in their lives becomes visible. This usually happens sometime during the first six months following the death. Now is the time when support is vitally important.

Continued Support

I recently saw a beautiful display of support when I went to mail a package. I was the second person in line, and while I waited for my turn, an elderly gentleman came into the mail service center. He shuffled slowly up to the side of the counter and stood there. The woman behind the counter gave him a big smile and in her heavy English accent said, "Good morning, love. How are you doing?" Then, she came out from behind the counter, while we all watched and waited, and gave him a big hug. They engaged in some small talk and then the gentleman shuffled back outside.

When it was my turn to be waited on, I simply could not resist asking about what had just taken place.

"Oh, that nice gentleman and his wife used to come in here all the time," she told me. "His wife died a couple of months ago. He only lives a few blocks from here so he comes by every day and we hug him."

What a rare display of compassion! I was really impressed. Too bad there isn't a "hug store" where people could all go when they are badly in need of comfort! The hugs and encouragement from a friend during this period of time help fill the void left after a loved one dies.

Encouragement

Encouragement might mean listening to "tapes" being played about the deceased, even if you have heard them many times before. It might mean understanding the overwhelming loneliness that is settling in, and trying to fill some of those empty hours with your presence. Or it might mean generously dispensing hugs.

The definition of the word encourage is, "to inspire with courage, spirit and hope."

Support may need to be offered as various guilty feelings begin to surface. To help work through these feelings, reassure the bereaved they did all they could. Use the phrase "the past cannot be changed, we can only plan for the future," until it becomes a refrain they repeat to themselves whenever guilty feelings creep into their thoughts. You may also offer support by gently steering the bereaved toward rewarding activities, without derailing the ongoing grief process.

Society's expectations are often unrealistic in regard to death. It takes careful observation and practice to gear responses to the needs of each individual. By doing so, you provide the best support possible in each person's case. When you begin to help someone who has suffered the loss of a loved one, you may feel awkward. Practice builds confidence and makes it easier. Each person who reaches out to sustain someone who is grieving is eventually one more person in our society who understands grief. A society educated in successful grief support would ease many an aching heart.

The importance society plays in the grieving process is made evident by this 86-year-old gentleman's story.

George

George joined our bereavement support group shortly before the six-month anniversary of his wife's death. He came to us extremely distraught because friends had been telling him he should be over the death of his wife by this time.

"We were married for 64 years," he told us. "Am I supposed to forget my life with her in a mere six months?" He wondered what was wrong with him because he still hurt so much and he wanted us to help him "get over it."

We explained that his well-meaning friends were not being realistic. How could they possibly expect him to no longer be mourning? Society often forgets that death is the end of a life, not the end of a relationship. The memories, the love and the time invested in that person never disappears.

We explained to George that it often makes friends uncomfortable to see someone despondent. They simply do not know how to deal with suffering. We then told him that he could cry and talk about his wife as much as he needed to when he was with us. It would not make us uncomfortable and it would certainly help him work through his grief.

He did just that. He cried copious tears that he had been holding back for the sake of others. And as a result of his participation in our group, he made a whole new circle of friends. All these friends were also grieving and better understood his situation. In each other, they found the understanding and support they lacked from their relatives and friends who did not understand grief and its process. This bereavement group went out for lunch, celebrated each other's birthdays and played bridge together. When someone was having a particularly bad day he or she would call another member of the group and ask for help.

The Grief Process Takes Time *and* Work

Grief does not automatically disappear with time. A friend tells me, "The passage of time does *not* heal. The task is one of courage, faith and the will to conquer. It is like the task of the disabled and the blind. There is no complete healing; there is only victory from molding the disaster into something that can help others."

Grief is work—hard work. It has to be talked out, cried out and acted out before changes can be made. This process takes time, and that is the reason society assumes that time heals the hurt. *In actuality, it is the work that takes place during the passage of time that eases the pain.* The lost loved one is never forgotten; the pain never completely disappears. However, as the grieving person adjusts to a new way of life, acceptance arrives. With acceptance, the agony eases gradually, until at last it is hardly noticed.

Grief does not automatically disappear with time. It takes time *and* work.

I have seen people five years after the death of a loved one who are still in acute, active grief. They were just beginning to face the loss and work it out after all that time. Time did not make the pain go away at all. Eventually, their grief had to be worked through or it would remain unresolved.

The Death of a Parent

I t has been brought to my attention, in confidential conversations with relatives, friends and acquaintances, that six months after a spouse has suffered the loss of a parent is a critical point in a marriage.

Support of a Spouse

Usually, in the early months after a loss, the spouse of the griever is understanding and supportive. After six months have passed, however, the griever is still seeking to be nurtured by his or her spouse, who by now has been completely drained. Remember: The spouse also has suffered a loss. Around six months, there is no longer a plentiful supply of sympathy to give out; the well has run dry. This can cause bad feelings between the couple as tensions mount. An irritable tone of voice creeps in, tempers are short and nothing seems to be right anymore.

> The six-month point after the loss of a parent can be a difficult time for marriages.

Many factors come into play. If the person whose parent has died experiences guilt over the neglect of his or her parent, the problem is magnified. If the spouse did not get along with the in-laws, that adds additional stress. If a lengthy illness prior to the death disrupted the family, more adjustment is needed. Occasionally, financial problems brought on by huge medical bills may arise.

Every relationship is different and complex and that makes it impossible to draw concrete conclusions. Nevertheless, realize that any of these situations can be explosive. Both the person whose parent died and their spouse may need our loving support.

Loss of a Second Parent

The loss of a second parent brings up an entirely new set of problems and circumstances. The family residence may have to be dismantled and sold. Years of memories may have to be disposed of in a matter of days. If the remaining family members are spread out all over the country, there is no time to clear out belongings in a leisurely way. My siblings and I emptied 50 years of accumulations in one short week. Decisions had to be made in a split second, and it was difficult to include everyone who may have wanted one of my mother's paintings or other special items. We did the best we could under the circumstances.

In many cases, all the siblings cannot be present to participate and feelings can get hurt. Relatives may not end up with the family treasure they so desired. Resentments can arise that may take years to resolve. If your spouse is grieving, and this was the case in his or her family, try to smooth over the rough spots and remember we all do the best we can during hurried and stressful situations. Try not to get in the middle of disagreements with relatives or siblings and remind yourself that this too will pass. Material belongings that seem terribly important immediately following a death have a way of diminishing in importance with time.

There is no easy answer about how to iron out the wrinkles in a marriage or family, except that, under these circumstances, time *does* have a way of helping. If your spouse is grieving, realize that six months is a short period of time with regard to grief. Extend your love and compassion a bit longer. You would not purposely want to add to your spouse's anguish. It may help to encourage your grieving partner to talk about his parents and to try to recall pleasant memories.

Remembering the Good Times

Sometimes, looking at childhood photographs can spark happy recollections. I had known my husband's parents for most of my life, so it was easy for me to recall happy memories. In cases where spouses have not known the in-laws for any length of time it is more difficult, and extra creativity is necessary. This is an especially important time to be a good listener.

Be aware that the six-month point can be a difficult time for marriages. It helps to be aware so you can be better prepared with your own family or with friends who have experienced the loss of a parent. By simply watching for problems, they can sometimes be avoided before they become serious. Understanding the basis of this winter season of grief can make it easier to await springtime.

Disposing of Belongings

O ur hospice team had a rule of thumb that we followed in regard to the disposing of personal belongings and clothing of the deceased. We felt it was best to begin the task during the first six months after a death or it was a sign of a potential problem.

Letting Go

During the first six months, the griever needs to think about the disposal of clothing and personal items. Tools that won't be used need to be given away or sold. If there is a car, camper, truck or boat that is no longer necessary, it needs to be put up for sale or given away. The slippers of the deceased should no longer be under the dining room table or the coat hung over the back of the hall chair. To have items like this around can indicate the griever expects the deceased to return.

Providing Incentive

If proper grief work has taken place, the bereaved have by this time accepted the fact that their loved one will not return home. If you do not see evidence of such acceptance, offer to help clear out a single closet and get the process started. Often, the grieving person has not begun the task because there is no incentive to do so. Provide incentive by suggesting a needy person or organization that would put the articles to good use. By offering to help with the task, you make it easier to begin. You can even be the one who physically removes the articles from the household, as long as the grieving person has taken part in sorting the items.

What to Keep

Photographs, souvenirs, memorabilia and even some clothing can certainly be kept. In fact, putting old photographs in albums can be a task that is very rewarding at this time. It helps the bereaved recall happy memories and rids their minds of the torment associated with a terminal illness or funeral, which otherwise might be the most vivid recent memories.

Putting old photographs in albums can be very rewarding.

Following the death of her husband, a 25-year-old widow found many positive ways to work out her grief, while at the same time preserving precious memories for her young children. The first thing she did was make a quilt for each child out of her husband's old flannel shirts. She told the children that when they missed Daddy they could wrap up in the quilt and pretend it was his loving arms.

She also made each child a photo album. She chose an extra-sturdy one that would survive the possibly rough use of small hands. Each album was different, with special pictures of that particular child with his or her father. She placed photos of her husband around the house and she mentions him frequently so her children remember him. She says it especially pleases her when one of her children remembers that Daddy loved waffles or some such thing.

Loneliness

A s we've seen, loneliness is very prevalent during the first six
months after a death. A caring friend spends time with the
bereaved person and includes him or her in family activities.
However, it is wise not to be too persistent if
the bereaved refuses an invitation. Once an
invitation has been extended, do not feel hurt
if it is turned down. The griever still
appreciates future invitations. Grieving
people feel different about what they are able
to participate in from day to day.

> Grieving people feel
> different about what
> they are able to
> participate in from
> day to day.

Social Obligations

You might advise grievers of their option to participate in social
activities or not, as they wish. Suggest that an easy way to do this
is simply to ask, "Can I get back to you on this?" whenever a
social obligation arises. Help grievers picture themselves in the
situation to decide whether it would be healthy for them to
participate. If they feel the situation would be too uncomfortable,
they must express this and politely refuse the invitation.

Allow Grievers to Say "No"

Betty told us that after her husband died, friends invited her to go
to his company picnic with them. She felt uncomfortable about it
and declined. The friends insisted she had always attended the
picnic and needed to go "for her own good."

She felt hesitant, knowing it would stir up memories of all the company picnics she and her husband had attended together. Her grief was fresh and raw and she felt terribly vulnerable. She knew she would be seeing her husband's colleagues for the first time since his funeral. The more she thought about it, the less she wanted to attend. She felt positive that refusing this invitation was the right thing to do. But her friends refused to take no for an answer.

The morning of the picnic, her friends arrived at her house and almost dragged her with them. They refused to listen to her repeated refusal to go to the picnic and even told her they had packed extra food especially for her. At last, she decided she had no choice but to join them. It was the worst day she had had since her husband died.

She cried and cried as she told us about it. Her intuition had told her not to go, but it took too much energy to be assertive against such strong competition. Betty's experience is a good reminder: We all need to be sensitive to the bereaved person's needs. Only that person knows what is best for him or her. By listening, you learn how to be of greatest help.

The Griever's Decision

That same day, we heard an unbelievably beautiful story from Ann, who had just returned from a month-long vacation. Prior to his death, Ann and her husband had been planning an extensive camping trip with close friends. Two months before the trip, Ann's husband suffered a fatal heart attack. Ann decided to make the trip anyway.

Everyone in our support group felt it would be a mistake and that she would be miserable visiting all the places she and her husband had mapped out together. But Ann had carefully considered all the pros and cons and decided to make the trip. We waited for her return with bated breath.

When she returned, all smiles, she reported that it had been a wonderful vacation. "Jim would have wanted me to go," she told us. The best part, however, had been her friends. They apparently were exceptionally special, sensitive people. They had talked frequently about Jim and had cried openly over their loss. As they shared golden memories, past and present, it had been almost as if Jim was on the trip with them. All this had been thoroughly therapeutic for Ann. She came home rested, relaxed and refreshed. Apparently, she had known what was the wisest choice and had taken it.

Dinner Invitations

Widows and widowers claim that dinnertime is the worst time of the day. As families gather together at the end of the day, the emptiness of their own home is jarring. They claim it is terribly depressing to prepare a meal for themselves and eat alone. Dinner invitations seem to be greatly appreciated, but are rarely extended.

Widowers frequently have a problem with cooking. In addition to meal invitations and taking food over to them, you may want to offer some cooking hints. A basic cookbook or assistance in simple meal preparation might be suitable and helpful.

> Widows and widowers claim that dinnertime is the worst time of the day.

In a microwave cooking class I took, I observed a daughter attending with her widowed father. They were both learning a method of cooking that would make meal preparation simpler. It was delightful to watch them together as she provided the opportunity for him to become more independent in his new life.

The Weekend

I am repeatedly told that the weekends seem to be the longest days in the week for people living alone. We advised our bereavement support group members to plan in advance for times that are the most difficult by planning an afternoon outing. Those of us who are not alone might want to look around our community to see who is alone and ask them to join our family gathering. During the grief process, it may take too much energy for the grieving person to reach out and mingle, so we need to extend our hands first.

In your desire to ease loneliness for grieving people, keep several points in mind:

- Each situation is different.

- Evaluate it before acting in a way that might add to the burdens the grieving person already carries.

- Respect the griever's decisions; don't be too forceful when an invitation is declined.

- Keep in mind that frequent cards, notes and phone calls let the bereaved know they have not been forgotten.

Forgiveness

son-in-law who brut
As friends of peop
need to tread ca
their anger.

Wh

U nresolved feelings of anger can add to a grieving person's loneliness. If you see your grieving friend clutching tightly to angry feelings and not moving toward forgiveness, cautiously try to ease this pain by suggesting he or she work out unresolved feelings with a counselor or through his or her religious practice.

When you approach this subject initially, you may be met with defensiveness and even more anger. However, the first seed has been sown. As time goes on, that seed can be watered with careful suggestions that promote growth toward forgiveness.

Open the Door to the Resolution of Anger

When working with grievers, I find that each suggestion about resolving anger I make is met with less resistance until finally the grievers reach the point where they think the idea of forgiveness originated within themselves. Sometimes a mere suggestion is adequate and they eagerly approach the subject of forgiveness on their own. I have seen many examples of forgiving and unforgiving grievers, and the positive effect forgiveness has on their recovery is remarkable.

It takes a vast amount of courage to forgive a person who has mortally wronged us. It takes the very best of a person to forgive the drunk driver who kills a 7-year-old only child or to forgive the

...lly murders his 20-year-old pregnant wife. ...e who have experienced such tragic losses, you ...refully and support them as they move beyond

Reaching Out

...en their only son was killed while riding his motorcycle, Lynn ...nd Bob were naturally devastated. A week later they began to think about the young man who had been driving the automobile that had hit their son. He had not been at fault, and no drugs or alcohol had been involved. It had been late at night with poor visibility when their son's motorcycle had pulled out in front of his car. Tire marks showed he had swerved to avoid the accident, but it had not been possible.

> With forgiveness comes an inner peace, an acceptance of what cannot be changed, a starting point for healing.

Bob told me, "One life was taken; we could not let this accident ruin another life. So we contacted the automobile driver and invited him to meet with us. We assured him that we did not blame him and that we wanted to help him forgive himself." Bob and Lynn were unusual in being able to approach this issue so soon after the death and in realizing they needed to do this.

When they met with the young man, all three cried together over what was such a sudden, meaningless loss. Three lives had been drastically changed in the split second it took for the accident to occur. Now all they wanted was to work together to ease each other's pain. They have kept in touch since the accident, filling a need in each other's lives as healing slowly continues.

Unresolved negative emotions cause distress, prevent inner healing and are a roadblock to true progress. No joy can flow through this roadblock. With forgiveness comes an inner peace, an acceptance of what cannot be changed, a starting point for healing.

Dan

Another example of forgiveness that I observed involved Dan, whose wife was murdered by her ex-husband. The day I met Dan he was seething with rage. Whenever he mentioned the murderer, his face changed dramatically. I knew the only way Dan was going to have any quality of life was if he could forgive his wife's murderer. Yet I knew in my heart that was an almost impossible task.

I'm a great believer in the power of prayer, so with folded hands I called out to God to find a way for Dan to heal. Two days later my telephone rang. It was Dan. "How are you?" I asked. "Just great," Dan responded. I had come to be satisfied if he answered, "OK." But I had never before heard him answer, "Just great."

When I recovered from my shock, I asked for an explanation. Dan explained that a gradual feeling of peace had come over him. He began to think about the murder and realized his wrath and vengefulness had disappeared; it had simply evaporated. I often had seen results to prayer, but it had never been so fast!

Dan went on to tell his story and to share the difference in his life after he was able to forgive. In the years since his loss, he has relocated, remarried and now leads support groups for survivors of violent deaths.

Holidays

Holidays are another time when loneliness takes hold. As holidays approach, they bring an extra layer of isolation for grieving people. In fact, holidays seem to be one of the largest obstacles on the path to recovery. Weeks or even months in advance of a holiday, stores display cards and signs that announce its arrival. It is impossible for a grieving person to shut out the fact that this is the first Father's Day they are facing without a father to phone, the first Christmas without that special person to shop for or the first Valentine's Day without a sweetheart.

How to Help with Holiday Plans

Every holiday brings with it many choices and decisions. Do I put up a Christmas tree? Do I still have the whole family over for dinner? How will I handle decorations by myself? Should I decorate the grave on the Fourth of July? So many decisions, at a time when the griever cannot even decide what to fix for dinner!

Allow the griever to talk about the approaching holiday and help him or her with these various choices. Allow the bereaved the freedom to do what is best in his or her particular situation. If chores are too overwhelming to be done alone, you can help.

The first Christmas after Elaine's husband died, she could not even think about a Christmas tree, so her son-in-law bought one

---

Allow the griever to talk about the approaching holiday. Help him or her with these various choices.

---

and set it up. Getting out the ornaments and putting lights on the tree seemed overwhelming, so there the unadorned tree sat. A friend stopped by and noticed the bare tree, and thoughtfully offered to bring her children over that evening to help decorate it. The children had a great time seeing the different ornaments, and together they somehow managed to get the lights put on the tree. A difficult chore became easier with other people on hand to help.

New Traditions

Offer to make the holiday a little easier with more than just practical assistance. The emotional trauma involved with holidays is often more of a problem than putting up decorations. Listen to see where you can be the greatest help. Old traditions are destroyed and new ones have not yet been established. Can you help start a new tradition that will bring comfort for years to come?

Along with traditions come the dreaded invitations. Some people simply want to be alone on holidays. If that is the case, respect their wishes. Dorothy told us that the Christmas after her son died, she was invited to her cousin's house for the holiday season. He lived across country and thought a change of scene might be good for her. She refused at first, but he insisted she not spend the holidays alone, so she boarded the plane apprehensively.

Dorothy said she felt uncomfortable the entire week, pretending she was having a good time. She knew her relatives meant well and she did not want to ruin the holiday for anyone else, so she tried to put up a good front. It took tremendous effort on her part.

The following year, when she was invited back, she gently explained that she planned to stay at home alone for the holidays. She was grateful for the invitation, but was even more grateful when her cousin said he understood. She was given the freedom to choose the way she would spend her day without being made to feel guilty. She confided in us that she was happier at home with a good book and a frozen dinner than having to wear a façade of good cheer.

Thoughtful Gestures

A phone call, note, card or meal invitation on any holiday—even insignificant ones—is greatly appreciated by the bereaved. Personal holidays, such as the birthday of the deceased, the birthday of the grieving person, anniversaries or any other day that was special are made a little easier if they are shared with or remembered by an encouraging friend.

Remembering that it has been six months since the death with a phone call or card sent to arrive on that date is also appreciated. Grieving people are unusually aware of significant dates.

> A phone call, note, card, or meal invitation on any holiday, even insignificant ones, are greatly appreciated by the bereaved.

I called my mom on my dad's birthday the first year after he had died. I had not planned to mention the date unless she mentioned it first, but I wanted to talk to her that day. She answered the phone and as soon as she heard my voice, inquired, "Do you know what today is?" Seldom does the grieving person forget. However, Mom had very cleverly set up a lunch date with several lady friends and planned to have dinner with my sister. "I'm not going to just sit home and feel gloomy today," she informed me. Good for her!

Offering Guidance

T he six-month anniversary can also be a time when it may be necessary to be firm. As a caring friend, you naturally want to be understanding and supportive of the grieving person. However, there are rare exceptions when the grieving person becomes manipulative. These cases must be dealt with in a different manner if the griever is to make progress.

How to Really Help

Richard was a good example of someone who needed less pampering. He was a strong, healthy 70-year-old man. Richard spent several years caring for his terminally ill wife before her death. When she died, he was left with no remnants of a life of his own. He paced and wrung his hands while big tears ran down his cheeks. Friends and neighbors rallied forth following his wife's death. They took him shopping, cleaned his house and invited him over for dinner. They almost smothered him with attention because he looked so pathetic.

After a few months of this tender loving care, the friends gradually withdrew their support because Richard appeared to be doing quite well. He was attending our bereavement support group, was learning to cook and had even planted a garden. Then, all of a sudden, he regressed back to crying, wringing his hands and refusing to attend our group. He complained that it was too depressing to eat alone, so he stopped eating entirely. He even threatened to commit suicide.

Immediately, friends and neighbors came forward. They took his hand and led him over to their homes for dinner. Richard thrived until the support lessened. This happened several times until the friends and neighbors became weary and called our agency for advice.

Discouraging Negative Behavior

Our consulting therapist explained that the well-meaning neighbors were reinforcing Richard's negative behavior. Richard found it more productive *not* to recover from his grief because he was taken care of when he appeared helpless. A pattern was developing that needed to be broken. Of course, nobody wanted to be cruel and reject his calls for help.

First they had to be sure he was not truly needy. Our therapist, who observed that when Richard was getting his own way, he was cheerful and happy, confirmed this. When left to his own resources, he reverted back to crying, refusing to eat and literally wringing his hands. We told his neighbors that this was the time to gently help him stand on his own.

If you see a negative pattern forming, suggest the griever seek professional help.

Supporting Constructive Behavior

We suggested they praise and support Richard when he made constructive accomplishments, instead of only coming to his aid when he was depressed. This was difficult, and many times his friends regressed. Nevertheless, eventually this special treatment paid off and Richard was able to drive himself to the store, invite friends to his house for dinner and feel more positive about his life. At the same time, he was working through his grief, instead of manipulating people.

If you see a negative pattern forming, suggest the griever seek professional help. Offer to call to set up an appointment, and even provide transportation. You may also want to seek professional advice on how to deal with these people to assist in their recovery.

Bereavement Support Groups

B ereavement support groups are usually advertised in the newspaper, and are sponsored by local hospitals or hospice organizations. You can make inquiries about the group, and offer to attend with the bereaved person the first time or two. Many of our members were brought to our group for the first time by someone who had attended the group previously, a hospice volunteer or a friend. The decision to attend a bereavement support group may be too difficult for a griever to do on his or her own.

Bereavement support groups are usually advertised in the newspaper, and are sponsored by local hospitals or hospice organizations.

Group situations are not for everyone, but they are always worth a try. I have found grievers progress quickly in a nurturing, compassionate atmosphere. It always warmed my heart to see the caring that went on between members of our group. No matter how intense their own pain, most people would reach out and put their arm around the person next to them to provide comfort. As they looked away from their own pain, it began to diminish.

Once, at the conclusion of a series of meetings, our group decided to go out for lunch together. We planned it carefully, and called it "Our Grand Finale." We reserved a long table at a local restaurant and it did not occur to us how much fun we were actually having until our waitress remarked on it.

"Boy, you guys sure know how to have a good time," she said. "What kind of group is this?" We burst out in spontaneous laughter. Yes, these grievers had come a long way together. Nevertheless, we didn't think this was a group that the waitress would want to join!

PART 4

The One-Year Anniversary

A New
Way of Life

A person who is grieving still has a hollow place in his or her heart and life after a year, but hopefully some positive changes and adjustments have taken place. As a caring friend, you have been offering encouragement all year long.

The One-Year Anniversary

The one-year anniversary date of a death is a milestone. Each holiday, birthday and anniversary has been faced during that year. The income-tax form, bank statements and finances have all been sorted out. The oil in the car has been changed, new holiday traditions begun and buttons sewn on the jacket. In other words, a new way of life, filled with many changes, has been adopted.

> The one-year anniversary date of a death is a milestone.

When I asked grieving people to tell me what they appreciated most at the end of the first year, they listed three things:

- assistance in practical matters

- mention of their loved one

- physical presence of caring friends or family

Practical Matters

I was told that the assistance in practical matters that was offered immediately following the death usually ceased by the one-year mark. Nevertheless, this was the time when help would have been greatly appreciated. Many items needed to be repaired and practical tasks needed to be figured out for the first time. A simple chore like changing a light bulb can overwhelm a person who is grieving. Many widows have told me that people offered help, yet never followed through. These empty offers seemed to hurt more than no offers at all.

A widow from one of our groups shared an example of a positive way to give assistance. She said that the day after Christmas, a young couple from her church appeared at her door. The man said, "I got a new saw for Christmas. Is it okay if I try it on that wood you have out back?" While he cut the wood, his wife sat in the kitchen and visited. After they had finished and gone home, the widow looked outside and to her amazement every log had been cut into small pieces, just the right size for her to handle.

Her eyes filled with tears as she shared this story. "I appreciated the kind way in which that help was offered. It didn't make me feel needy or inadequate. The young man almost made it sound like I was doing him a favor by letting *him* cut my wood with his new saw." A thoughtful task of this type appears to be the most appreciated.

Mentioning the Loved One

Remembering to mention the loved one who has died is especially important, even after a year. So often, grievers feel that nobody remembers their loved ones, misses them or cares about them any longer. One woman said she was especially touched by her pastor who, as he struggled with the movie projector, muttered, "Where's Ray when I need him?" She said her husband had always been the church member who came to the rescue when they had mechanical problems, and she was delighted to know he had been appreciated and was missed.

Letters are wonderful ways to uplift a grieving person. Almost a year after my father died, I received a letter from a friend of his. I had never met the man, but I had heard Dad speak of him often. He wrote that he could picture my dad in heaven organizing committees to accomplish great feats. This made me smile because Dad had truly been a great organizer. He wrote several other clever anecdotes, including the fact that everything in heaven was now done in triplicate. Dad thought if one of something was good, three were better! And he closed by telling me that I had inherited my writing ability from my dad and that he lives on in everything I write. I had not looked at it that way before.

> Letters are wonderful ways to uplift a grieving person.

In addition to my being a writer, all three of my daughters are talented writers. Recently, 11 years after Dad's death, my first grandson, Matthew, won an Author-of-the-Month award in his first-grade class. How I wish I could have shared this with Dad. However, our family is pleased with the legacy he has left for many generations to come. If it had not been for that particular letter from one of my dad's caring friends, I might never have made the connection of our common legacy.

That letter probably took less than an hour to write, but years later I still cherish it. It did not just contain meaningless sentimentality; it contained personal comments that brought Dad back to me for a little while and made me smile over the endearing personality traits that were unique to him.

Acknowledging the Anniversary

Around the actual date of the death, one year later, most grieving people relive all the events that took place the previous year. At noon, they remember they were dressing for the funeral service and at 3:00 P.M. they were standing by the graveside. Even if they were in a state of complete shock, they still seem capable of bringing up emotions to the surface, experiencing the intense anguish they had felt the previous year.

The physical presence of someone who cares to share in the actual anniversary date is very important. A sympathetic friend could suggest an activity for this date that would commemorate the sad occasion in a suitable manner. Some appropriate activities might include having family members attend a religious service together, share a meal or gather friends and family to plant a tree or flowers at the gravesite. The Jewish tradition gathers loved ones together on the one-year anniversary date to go to the cemetery to place a headstone on the grave. In this way, loving support is available when it is most needed.

If it is not possible to be physically present with the grieving person, a single rose delivered to the home of the bereaved can bring great comfort. Any action that lets the grievers know that they are not suffering alone, and that there are other people who care and who miss the same loved one, provides comfort.

Change in Residence

Often, people begin to think about changing their residence by the one-year anniversary date. This is frequently decided from a financial standpoint or to be closer to family members.

Living Arrangements

Widows may prefer to live in condominiums or apartments where maintenance is done for them. Mobile homes and retirement villages are popular for elderly people because they feel safer than living alone and it offers an opportunity to become part of a small community. People living in the country may wish to move into town for safety and convenience.

The bereaved has had a year to think about moving and can choose wisely at this point. Moving before the first year is completed is usually discouraged. When acute grief work is going on, it is too difficult to make wise decisions.

> Moving before the first year is completed is usually discouraged. When acute grief work is going on, it is too difficult to make wise decisions.

A Helping Hand

If the move is decided upon after a year, you can enthusiastically help your friend with the entire process. Working together to put shelf paper in the kitchen cabinets is much more fun than doing it alone. Choosing carpet or wallpaper often requires a second opinion. You can stand by the grieving person's side, and help make his or her change in residence easier and more enjoyable. The move may also precipitate the final cleaning out of the garage or closets and disposing of the remnants of the loved one's belongings. This chore, too, is easier when shared.

Moving On

With a change in residence, many unhappy memories can be put aside. A home holds so many memories, both good and bad. Frequently, a fresh start for a griever can only begin in a new residence. In a new home, the griever no longer has to face the special bedroom that belonged to the deceased or the room their loved one may have died in. They won't have the garden they planted with their spouse, or the home that held so many plans for the future that became lost dreams after the death. They can leave behind the prospective nursery that is a constant reminder as long as it remains empty.

If a grieving person talks about a change in residence, you can encourage him or her, but be careful not to force the decision.

> If a grieving person talks about a change in residence, you can encourage him or her, but be careful not to force the decision.

To uproot a widow, talk her into selling the home she has lived in for 30 years and move her into another relative's home is not usually a good idea. Both the positive and negative aspects of the move need to be examined carefully. The bereaved person must make the final choice.

Dot and her mother are typical examples of a move gone awry. Dot was an only child. When her father died, she insisted her mother sell her house on the East Coast and move in with her. Dot reasoned that the California climate would be easier for her mother to cope with than the severe eastern winters. Dot had an extra bedroom and she and her husband were eager for Dot's mother to be with them. They would no longer have to worry about her living alone, so far away. They helped her sell her home and all the furnishings.

Change in Residence
Can Cause Illness

According to medical experts, any change in residence is traumatic and can result in illness. This is true even when the move is eagerly anticipated. Keep a sharp eye on the newly relocated person and watch for such illnesses.

However, Dot's mother was not happy in California. She missed her senior citizen's group and her church work. She missed having her own home and garden to putter around in. She felt like a perennial guest who did not belong. Dot finally had to move her into her own apartment on the East Coast, but of course they could never replace all of her belongings.

A Positive Move

Contrary to this unfortunate situation was Gail who, after considerable deliberation, sold her home and moved into a condominium. I visited her on the year anniversary date of her husband, Bob's, death. I was anxious to see how she was adjusting. When I went to her new home, I was startled to see an entirely new look. She had changed her accent color from blue to a dusty mauve and it looked lovely.

She laughed when I remarked on it. "I have always loved mauve," she told me, "but Bob hated it. It dawned on me just before I moved that I could have all the mauve I wanted in my new home!" She went on to tell me, in a whisper, that she had even treated herself to a new negligee in matching mauve. I was so pleased to see Gail actually joke about this. It showed tremendous progress in the acceptance of a new way of life. She had found some advantages to living alone and was concentrating on the positive aspects rather than the negative ones.

Other Changes

M ost change is a sign of progress and moving forward. A change in residence, changes in traditions and a general reorganization most likely occurred during the first year. If these changes were successful, they have become the "new normal." If they were unsuccessful, more experimentation will have to take place until satisfactory solutions are reached. As a supportive friend, you can help with these decisions. You can be a sounding board while the grieving person tries to make changes.

How to Be a "Sounding Board"

When listening to a griever work through change, remember two main ideas:

Advice is not necessary. Merely listening as people come to their own conclusions is more helpful than giving advice. Even more helpful is to apply sensitive and reflective listening skills as ideas are forming and decisions are being made.

Applaud positive changes. They reinforce the desire to re-establish a meaningful existence. Frequent experimentation may be necessary before a new way of life is established.

Signs of Acceptance

Women often begin their acceptance and adjustment process with outward signs of changes in their appearance, such as a new outfit, a new hairstyle or a new hair color. Gently suggest these changes and offer to join a visit to a hair salon or a trip to a city shopping mall to choose some new clothes. It is sometimes easier to do these things in the company of a friend.

Men often grow beards, mustaches or buy a new car as they venture into their new life. They may appreciate help in practical matters, such as cooking and doing the laundry, rather than in experimenting with their physical appearance. Each person and each situation is different, but by listening carefully, you can ascertain the best way to support an individual's healing process, even after a year.

One of the most helpful ways for grievers to complete their healing is through reaching out to others as they adapt to a "new normal" way of life.

Reaching Out

T he final step in healing from a loss is made by reaching out to others. However, often it is difficult for the bereaved to reach out by themselves. This is where a friend can help. You can look for areas that would be interesting to the bereaved person and then offer to join these activities.

Shared Activities

If physical exercise is an area that appeals to a particular person, suggest taking a class together. Obtain the information and jointly register for the class. If learning a new skill is of interest, make some phone calls, compile a list of available classes in the community, and then volunteer to participate in the activity with your grieving friend. This skill can be something creative like a ceramics class, a tole painting class or a college writing course.

If structured, scheduled activities seem unappealing to the grieving person, it may be more helpful to be on hand for an occasional game of tennis, a walk in the park or a luncheon date instead. Whatever activity is appropriate, it is easier for the griever to participate when he or she doesn't have to do it alone.

Volunteering

Volunteers are becoming scarce in all aspects of society. As a result, most religious organizations, groups and communities have great unfulfilled needs. A few phone calls can be made to establish a list of available places where help is needed.

The Comfort of Children

Parents who have suffered the loss of a child often wish to work with children to fill the void. One young mother started a day-care center so she could fill her arms with cuddly babies and her ears with the sound of children's laughter. A father volunteered for the Big Brother program and spent his quiet Saturday afternoons throwing a softball to a fatherless boy. Their *own* pain lessened when they reached out. Encourage the griever to reach out.

Sharing the Wisdom

As a caring friend, you can encourage grievers to reach out to others who share the same grief they have experienced. The kindred spirit between two mothers suffering the loss of a child, or two widows helping each other adjust to a life alone can be a soothing balm. A person who has grieved, cried and experienced such depth of sadness can truly help others who experience similar hurts. A griever's wisdom, gained from his or her season of tears, guides him or her to sympathize with and heal broken hearts.

> Grievers benefit from reaching out to other grievers.

It has been proved that grievers benefit from reaching out to other grievers. I never hesitate to put grievers in contact with each other. Nevertheless, I am sure to wait until enough time has elapsed so that the encounter does not drag the experienced griever down.

This does not mean the bereaved should burden a newly grieving person with his or her own tales of grief. It means they can put the anguish of their own losses to good. In using the empathy, sensitivity and understanding they wished others had used with them, they can serve a great need. At the same time, grievers hasten their own recovery by reaching out to others.

Hope

Susan told me she had many visitors following the death of her husband. She appreciated them all, but admitted the most comfort came from Marlene, who had been widowed two years before.

She said, "Marlene knew all the right things to tell me. She told me to go ahead and cry and that my pain was understandable. She did not tell me to 'cheer up' or that 'time would make everything better.'"

Susan could look at Marlene and see her healthy glow. She could see her smile as they held hands. She could see living evidence that another widow had recovered, and it offered hope that she, too, would recover someday.

Delayed or Displaced Grief

U p to this point, we have discussed *normal* grief. Occasionally, a situation does not fit the norm. A person who was unable to grieve at the time of the death may show signs of extreme grief at a much later date. This is not a matter to be concerned about. Grief, worked out at anytime, is better than grief left unresolved. I have seen several classic cases of *delayed grief* and *displaced grief.*

Delayed Grief

One came about as a result of Bob's relatives keeping him overly busy traveling and visiting immediately following his wife's death. He came to us experiencing delayed grief. When he returned home after his travels many months later, the empty house hit him with a force that almost destroyed him.

While Bob had been traveling, he had not faced the reality of his wife's absence. He could still picture her at the kitchen sink and sitting in her favorite chair in front of the television set. When he arrived home, he was forced to face the fact that she no longer physically shared his life. Her clothes were still hanging in the closet, her toothbrush was in the bathroom, but she was no longer there.

> If you see a situation of delayed grief, help the way you would have right after the death occurred.

As he reached out for support, he could not find any. Friends and neighbors thought that by this time "he would be over it." No meals were brought over. No offers to accompany him to the bank were forthcoming. He was on his own—all alone. Fortunately, he found his way to our bereavement support group, and the other members reached out to help him begin his walk along the path of recovery. They allowed him a season of tears that would eventually produce a crop of sensitivity and caring for others.

If you see a situation of delayed grief, come forward and help the way you would have right after the death occurred. You might also be able to enlist the aid of others who didn't recognize the delayed need.

Unresolved Grief

Another case of delayed grief I saw involved a mother whose 12-year-old son had been killed in an accident. The mother had been studying to become a registered nurse. After her son's death, she continued to attend classes and amazed everyone with her capacity to function. After graduation, she began to work at a local hospital. She came to see us because she was being transferred to the pediatric-oncology ward and realized she could not face working with children.

She was at last confronting her unresolved grief and knew it had to be dealt with before she could function properly. She took a three-month leave of absence from work, attended our group, went into private therapy and finally cleared out her son's belongings. In the beginning, we observed that she could not sit still in her chair. I have never seen a person in such constant motion. She twisted, turned, swung her foot. She was a tightly strung top just waiting to spin out of control. When she spoke, her words came out fast and furious. When she cried, she sobbed from the depths of her soul.

> Delayed grief can be more visible and intense than normal grief. It is more difficult to deal with, but very necessary.

Six months later, I was pleased to see the success of her various efforts. She sat calmly, with a smile on her face. She shared with us the anguish and despair she had experienced in those six months. She had worked hard to overcome her grief, but she reassured us that it had been well worth the effort and pain. She was looking forward to her new career and felt a peace she had not had in her life up to this point. She was making plans to work with the parents of her pediatric patients to help them understand the care of terminally ill youngsters. She hoped to use the death of her son to develop an inner strength that would enable her to help others.

Delayed grief can be more visible and intense than normal grief. It is more difficult to deal with, but is necessary to experience. Watch for signs of delayed grief when you see normal grief stages being bypassed. Eventually, the grief will erupt and the person will need the help of a caring friend or relative to work through it.

Displaced Grief

Like delayed grief, displaced grief is uncommon, but it does sometimes occur. You may see a person who stood tall and strong at the funeral of their own loved one, crying uncontrollably at the funeral of a distant relative. You may see someone unable to attend a memorial service out of the belief "it would be too difficult to face the widow." Displaced grief can hit unexpectedly and seem completely out of proportion to the situation.

> Displaced grief needs to be looked at carefully by friends and family. If it seems to be out of proportion to the situation or goes on for a lengthy time, suggest professional help.

I saw a classic case of displaced grief when I attended a funeral with Debbie. She had been the volunteer on a hospice case for an exceptionally lovely family and the staff all wanted to show their support by going to the funeral. As soon as the soloist began to sing, Debbie began to cry. By the time the song was finished, she was sobbing almost uncontrollably. She made a quiet exit from the back of the church straight into the bathroom. I followed her because she looked like she needed to be comforted.

"I don't know what came over me," she stammered, as she mopped tears off her face. "This is so strange and unlike me. I didn't shed a tear at my father's funeral six months ago even though I was so close to him. I wonder what happened?"

I didn't wonder a bit. As I consoled Debbie, I reminded her that her tears could be a sign of delayed and displaced grief. The crying was necessary for her grief process. I gently asked if her tears might be needed to wash away any lingering hurt that hadn't been released at her father's funeral.

She nodded. "I didn't allow myself to cry at my father's funeral because I knew how much it would upset my younger sisters. I thought I would save it for when I got home, but by then I no longer felt like crying—until today, that is."

The crying episode had been good for Debbie. However, displaced grief needs to be looked at carefully by friends and family. If it seems to be out of proportion to the situation or goes on for a lengthy time, suggest professional help.

Listening to
Your Heart

J ane told us that a year after her husband died, she began to
feel as if she were losing her mind. She had been through so
many experiences during the first year that at times it was
overwhelming. For several days, she kept having thoughts about
her sanity that plagued her. It reached an almost unbearable fear
around 8:00 P.M. one evening, just as the phone rang.

A friend apologetically said, "Jane, this may sound funny to
you, but I keep getting the idea to call you and tell you that you
are not going crazy." She explained she had hesitated to call, but
the intuitive message was loud and clear. She laughingly added,
"I guess you could say that I'm just following orders. Is there
anything I can do for you?"

Jane sighed with relief. There was nothing more she needed
from this friend. She had brought the ultimate comfort with her
call and message.

I believe God knows all about suffering and works in His
own mysterious ways to send help. When my mother died, I
notified the out-of-town relatives. When I called my cousin Joseph
in Boston, he hesitated and said he would call me back. When he
called back, he said he and his fiancé, Virginia, would like to fly
into Chicago for the funeral.

I had never met Virginia and knew that Joseph lives on an
extremely limited income, so I tried to convince him it was not

necessary. We all knew he cared and it was enough to have made the offer. Still Joseph, in his deep, quiet voice insisted, "Virginia and I will arrive on Friday night." Although his offer and effort touched me, I felt it was placing an unnecessary burden on him to attend.

My husband and I picked up Joseph and Virginia at the airport and there was an instant bond between Virginia and me. I have always had a special place in my heart for Joseph and she jumped right into my heart beside him. She did not let go of my hand as we walked to the parking lot.

I found myself pouring out my heart to her while Joseph and my husband talked man-talk. All the pent-up feelings I had been protecting my siblings from spewed forth. When I finished, I felt unburdened, at peace and ready to face the funeral the next day. Virginia continued to be a terrific support system for me the entire weekend and has remained one of my best long-distance friends and support system in the years since then.

The most interesting part of this story is that I later found out Virginia is a trained counselor. I had my own private therapy sessions all weekend! Joseph and Virginia heard God telling them to come to Chicago and they followed His instructions.

Over the years I have had many personal experiences of a smaller magnitude when I was the one who felt led to go to some unusual place or to undertake an unlikely task. This no longer surprises me and I have learned to trust my heart. I often want to ignore these signs because they seem a bit foolish or odd.

However, I try to stop whatever I am doing and reach for the telephone or a pen to write a note. I have never been disappointed by the recipients' reactions. People think I have blessed them, when in actuality, I have received an even greater blessing. I heartily agree with Ralph Waldo Emerson, who said, "It is one of the most beautiful compensations of this life that no man can sincerely try to help another without helping himself."

Comfort Measures

✦

E ven a year after a major loss, people who have suffered continue to need consolation. There are many simple methods that help return a feeling of peace and good will to a griever's life. The following methods can also be incorporated into a caregiver's life to help him or her remain in good shape.

Sleep

One method is to help improve sleep habits. Often, grievers sleep poorly, tossing and turning and waking up numerous times. Experts agree that sufficient sleep is vital to good health and the quality of life. Poor sleep habits reduce energy levels, lower mental and social functioning, and in general adversely impact lives.

If your friend shows any indications of poor sleep habits, you can offer to fill in while your friend takes a nap. If there are young children in the home, you might offer to take them to the park for a few hours to ensure a quiet house that is conducive to napping. Even short naps can restore a feeling of well-being.

You can also remind the griever of factors that interfere with good nighttime sleep habits. Good sleep habits, as listed by the National Sleep Foundation, are:

- Avoid alcohol, caffeine, nicotine and decongestants.

- Don't exercise or eat heavy meals just before bedtime.

- Go to bed and wake up at the same time every day.

- Try not to focus on your worries before bedtime.

Aromatherapy

Another good way to soothe away stress is with aromatherapy. The practice of aromatherapy has become popular to calm an over-stressed society. Check almost any store and you will find lotions, soaps, candles and bath products especially formulated to produce a calming effect. Fragrances such as chamomile, lavender, freesia, mimosa and jasmine are only a few that can be purchased. My daughter Sheryl often fixes me a basket of bath products, attractively tied up with ribbon and net. She also buys me delicious-smelling candles that I keep around my bathtub for sweet-smelling, relaxing bathtimes. Nothing makes me feel more pampered. The products last for months and make me grin when I use them.

A small gift that has a soothing or calming effect is a thoughtful gesture and lets your friend or loved one know you care about his or her welfare.

Likewise, fragrances from food can be comforting. Who can resist the aroma of fresh-baked bread? How about homemade chocolate-chip cookies warm from the oven? Don't they make you feel loved? Even a bag of oranges with their pungent smell can evoke memories and act as a natural antidepressant. Our sense of smell evokes memories of happier times and can play an important role in offering solace.

This is a good time to present a small gift that has a soothing or calming effect. It is a thoughtful gesture and lets your friend or loved one know you care about his or her welfare. A year may have gone by since the loss occurred, but there is still a need for encouragement.

Healing Sounds

Our sense of hearing can be another means of bringing comfort. A pleasant tape or CD that can be played when nerves feel frazzled is a thoughtful gift and also a helpful one. It helps the griever know someone cares.

Silence

On the other hand, the precious sound of silence plays an important role too. Ours is a society that has constant noise. Even in a house with the television or CD player turned off, there are still noises. I hear the refrigerator cycle off and on, the computer humming and the washer and dryer working in the other room. The air conditioner cycles all summer and the heater all winter. I hear cars, leaf blowers and the street cleaner.

Living in the desert, I frequently hear the sound of the wind whistling through my house. Stores, restaurants and most business offices have music playing constantly, often with the volume turned way up. And I just read that in Southern California even cemeteries are beginning to pipe in music!

Silence is important to anyone's well-being, but especially that of grievers. Their minds are deluged with details and questions. To sort out their inner turmoil, they need quiet. Offer to help find a way or a place for the griever to satisfy his or her need for quiet.

Laughter and Fun

Strange as it may sound in a book about grief, laughter is necessary for balance while grieving. Find ways to release the griever's pent-up emotions through laughter. A light, humorous book with cartoons that can be picked up when things get too heavy is an excellent choice. Or suggest going to a movie theater that is showing something suitable. Be sure your friend is in on the choice so you do not appear to be heartless or frivolous in the midst of his or her pain.

Grievers are often embarrassed when they catch themselves having a good time. They think people will feel they have forgotten their loss or do not care about the deceased person any longer. This is false thinking. Nobody can grieve 24 hours a day, every single day. Everyone needs a break. Just as a man carrying a heavy burden must put down his load occasionally to rest, so must grievers set aside their heavy burden of grief and take a rest now and then. You can be that person who helps them set down their burden and rest. Then, you can continue with them along their journey toward complete healing.

Chapter 33

Long-Distance Help

W hen your grieving friends or relatives live a great distance from you and you cannot reach out physically to help or hug them, what can you do? You can telephone, you can write letters and you can find creative ways to help.

Phone Calls

Long-distance phone calls can often prove to be difficult. The grieving person may begin to cry, making conversation almost impossible. Simple, compassionate words can comfort the griever. "Just know I am thinking about you and that I care," is often all you need to say. The call need not be long. The phone call's purpose is just to let the person know you remember their loss and pain.

Notes and Letters

Sending notes or letters add a little joy to a griever's life. People tell me they like notes even better than flowers. Empty mailboxes are depressing. To find something with a familiar handwriting that says, "I'm thinking about you and I care," brings a smile to a solemn face. It takes little time to dash off a card and it can make a difference in an entire day for the recipient. A letter sharing a memory is even better.

After my mother died, I received a card from my cousin Susan, who lives in Texas. She added a handwritten note that said being with my parents had been similar to sitting in front of a cracking fireplace on a cold winter night. Wow! That summed it up completely. Anyone going into my parent's home instantly felt welcome. When they left, they felt warm, comforted and loved. Just a simple sentence, but one that brought a smile to my face and joy to my heart.

> Sending notes or letters add a little joy to a griever's life.

Unique Ways to Help

When my niece's husband drowned, Lisa was living far away in Texas. My heart went out to Lisa and I wanted to do something special to ease her pain. I was sure her phone was ringing off the hook those first few days and I hesitated to add any extra confusion to the situation. I sent messages through my sister, who kept me up-to-date on the arrangements.

I continued to think about ways I could be the most help. One day it came to me that I had file cabinets filled with information concerning loss from my many years in the field of hospice and grief. When I finally spoke to Lisa, I asked if she was up to doing any reading. Her enthusiasm was obvious. "Oh, Aunt June, that's all I do most of the day. I want to learn all I can so I can get through this and help my children." She didn't need to say anything else. I was on a mission.

I dug through my files, went to the library and researched newly released books. I headed to the bookstore and made copies and lists. I gathered everything I could find, then packed up a big box and mailed it. Lisa was quite appreciative and three years later I am still sending her any new material I find that I think will help.

Lisa's main concern was for her young children. She concentrated on dealing with her loss so she could rear them. "I don't want them to think they have a sad mommy," she told me. With a new baby and a 2-year-old, she knew how great her responsibilities were.

Unable to find a support group for young widows and widowers, she started her own. Three years later, she is still leading this group and making a difference in the lives of others. In reaching out to others, she benefited herself and received necessary comfort from others in a similar situation.

In Lisa's case, I knew cards and flowers would not be enough. I had to dig deeper and reach out in a more unique way to make a difference. Even a year later, remember people who are still mourning. Whatgifts or special talents do you have that could be used to ease another's pain?

> Reach out in unique ways to make a difference. What gifts or special talents do you have that could be used to ease another's pain?

Chapter 34

Self-Care

One extremely important way to help someone who is grieving is to keep yourself in top shape. A person who is grieving is often difficult to get along with and can be very wearing on the nerves. Grievers can play the same "tapes" repeatedly, seem to cry over nothing and demand your time when you least wish to be disturbed. Therefore, it is important to take time for yourself so you can be physically, emotionally and spiritually ready with the strength to overcome any obstacles that might otherwise stand in the way of your whole-hearted caring.

Time for Yourself

It is not selfish to take time to read a humorous book or to soak in a hot bubble bath. These are necessities that relax you and replenish your own natural reserves so you can share your time, energy and other resources whenever necessary. An empty pitcher does little to quench a person's thirst.

Also remember to eat properly, get enough sleep and take the time to exercise both your body and mind. Seek others with whom you can talk and be nourished by, so you are in the best possible shape to help others. It is much more difficult to listen patiently to a grieving friend when your own head is

> It is not selfish to take time to read a humorous book or to soak in a hot bubble bath. These are necessities!

throbbing with a headache because you did not take time to eat breakfast. It is also difficult to listen exclusively to depressing stories. However, when these experiences are balanced with good cheer and strong friendships, they are not as likely to drag you down.

Group Support for Caregivers

There is a special power in groups of all kinds. Bereavement support groups are recommended for the grieving, but the helpers also need group contact to give them extra sustenance for their job. For this reason, support groups for people in helping professions and for caregivers are popping up in many communities. If none is available in your area, form a support system of your own. Even meeting once a week for breakfast or lunch with a friend who can support and encourage you can be a great help.

Take a Break

When a situation seems to be getting too heavy to handle, in addition to outside support of some sort, a short respite can renew your strength. Arthur Gordon once said that salt water could cure anything, be it in the form of sweat, tears or the sea. I have thought about that solution and used it often. A workout, a walk along the beach or a good old-fashioned cry makes you a better helper.

Another method I use is to treat myself to a long, leisurely bubble bath every night. I fill my oversized bathtub with fragrant bubbles and I soak until my skin gets wrinkly. I look forward to these quiet times that relax and refresh me. You might find watching sports or digging in the backyard works for you.

Another of my secrets is that I refuse to watch any television or movies that contain violence or depressing themes. I seek out lighthearted comedies, the sillier the better, and fortunately, I have been blessed with a family that has a great sense of humor.

My husband, children, their spouses and my grandchildren fill our home with laughter. The fun we have together restores me so I am better able to face the outside world. And best of all, every couple of years I am presented with a new grandchild to cuddle and love. I know this treat will not go on indefinitely, but for now it is simply wonderful. To be able to kiss dimpled little hands and tickle chubby little feet restores me!

It's important never to get so involved in helping others that you neglect your own good mental and physical health. Without those strengths, you are unable to help in any capacity. When you take the time to replenish yourself, the help you give others is easy to give. Your attitude is fresh, and your capacity to love and support those in your life is strengthened.

The Future

T he death of a loved one can lower self-esteem, destroy self-confidence and deplete the grievers' energy. You can help by standing on the sidelines, allowing grieving people to draw on your self-esteem, confidence and energy for as much time as they need to replenish their own supply.

Remember that the second holiday season after the death is often worse than the first one. Family and friends who offered support the first year often do not realize it is also necessary the *second* year. Plans that were carefully made the first year seem unnecessary, so the second season often creeps up without an armor of protection to cushion the impact. A caring friend can serve as that armor of protection by helping the grieving person plan ahead.

Dating

Dating is another delicate issue. If widows or widowers begin dating, they are usually embarrassed to talk about their new social life with friends who knew their deceased spouse. Ease any discomfort they may have by encouraging them and supporting them as they move on. It is important that they know you are happy for them and will continue to be their friend. Reaching out to new people and experiences is a good sign. It's OK to let the bereaved know you realize the lost loved one is not forgotten, and that you know it means the bereaved person is adjusting successfully to his or her loss.

Progress

The rewards of watching the growth and progress of a griever are endless. To see a person in the lowest ebb of life go through a convalescent period, and eventually reach full recovery, is a miracle. By being a caring presence, you assist with this recovery. You are the one who helps them accomplish the necessary tasks. You provide warmth, courage and help fight off defeat. You nurture the grieving person, much as a gardener tends a precious plant.

You serve as the gardener who determines whether a plant lives and thrives—or withers on the stalk. A plant left uprooted or unattended becomes stunted, unattractive and robbed of its potential. This plant does not blossom nor bear fruit. However, with fertilizing, mulching, pruning and watering, this same plant enriches its surroundings with beauty and prolific fruit.

People who are grieving must be nurtured in much the same way. They need to be treated tenderly after being uprooted from their former lives. They need to be transplanted gently, nurtured and cared for with kindness. They need to be tended by a gardener who cultivates trust.

Producing fruitfulness takes love, labor, care and time. None of this happens overnight—with plants or people. To successfully tend grieving people, respect their individual rights, while at the same time be available to help. Like a good gardener, you can provide the necessary conditions for growth—and feel proud when you see them grow.

Epilogue

When my granddaughter Melody was 2-1/2 years old, she looked out the glass doors to our backyard. "What's that?" she asked. I was sitting in a rocking chair next to the door where I couldn't see outside. "That's the swimming pool," I answered. I figured Melody was looking at the pool.

She pushed her nose harder against the glass and repeated, "What's that?" I answered again, "A swimming pool." Little Melody frowned and we went through this exercise again—her voice louder this time.

I decided to go over to the door and look. Across from the pool was a windsock that was blowing furiously. Melody must have been looking at that and knew, for sure, it was not a swimming pool, California kid or not!

"Oh, honey, I'm sorry. That's a windsock you're looking at," I told her. "Come on, let's go look at it." I picked her up and we went outside for a closer look at the windsock. I stood underneath it, so that when the wind blew, the streamers trailed across her face. She wrinkled up her nose and giggled each time it touched her.

I took this opportunity to talk to her about feeling the wind even though she couldn't see it. "Love is like that, too," I told her. "We know people love us even when we can't see love with our eyes. We can feel it, like you are feeling the results of the wind right now." Love, the concern of others, peace and joy can be experienced, but not actually seen.

Peace, love and joy touch people who are grieving in much the same way as the windsock blew across Melody's face. She could not see what was moving the sock, but she could feel the results. Grievers cannot see where their touches of peace and joy come from either; they simply know they are there.

Before working with people who were grieving and suffering my own losses, I assumed that by a year after a death, the time of mourning would be complete. Now I realize this is not possible. The pain from the loss of a loved one never goes away completely. With time, and following intense grief work, there are long periods of time when the sadness is not present. But then an unexpected spasm of grief washes over us. *This is the price we pay for having loved someone. To never experience grief, we would have to never experience love.*

To help someone who is grieving, remember that grief goes on even after the first year. You can continue to share memories of the deceased as a way of acknowledging this loss in your own life. You can also continue to remember holidays and special days and the part the person who has died would have played in these events. You can continue to encourage the entire family whenever it is needed.

A friend's granddaughter was married a year after her father's death. She asked her grandfather to walk her down the aisle. She coped with her loss exceptionally well that day. My heart was touched as I realized how difficult this must have been for the entire family. However, as usual, I was pleased to see the resilience of the human spirit.

During the wedding reception, when the traditional dance between father and daughter would normally take place, this young woman danced with her grandfather. His wife told me he said to her, "It should be your dad out here, not me," to which she responded with a smile, "God had other plans for him." Life does go on and with good support, lots of love and God's help, it does become good again. How rewarding it is to hear stories like this about recovery in progress!

One of my most uplifting experiences began with an invitation written in an unfamiliar handwriting. With a puzzled look on my face, I opened it as I walked back to my house from the mailbox. It was from a widow who had been in one of our bereavement support groups two years before. Apparently, the group still continued to meet socially and they wanted me to join them for their two-year reunion dinner. I was delighted.

That evening I walked into a roomful of strangers. These could not possibly be the same people I had met two years ago! Those people had faced me with tears in their eyes, not smiles on their faces. This group was meticulously groomed, relaxed and friendly. I remembered the tension I had felt as I walked into the room at our meetings and the way the people would sit stiffly in their chairs with folded arms or clenched fists.

After exchanging hugs, I sat down to join this group. What a wonderful time I had that night! We shared numerous stories. We discussed local news topics and occasionally someone would mention their lost loved one—not with sadness, but with acceptance. We smiled over one woman having to climb up on her roof to nail down shingles after a bad windstorm and about our 86-year-old gentleman clumsily changing a light bulb and falling off a stepladder in the process. Amazingly, he was completely unharmed from the fall. The point of sharing these stories showed that practical tasks were no longer a problem. These people were functioning successfully in all areas.

I drove home from that reunion with a light heart. I had received the best possible gift. I had been able to see an entire group of people who had come full circle in their grief work. It encouraged me to continue with my work and to write this book.

Bill of Rights for the Bereaved

1. Do not make me do anything I do not wish to do.

2. Let me cry.

3. Allow me to talk about the deceased.

4. Do not force me to make quick decisions.

5. Be patient with me even when my behavior appears strange.

6. Let me see that you are grieving too.

7. When I am angry, do not discount it.

8. Do not speak to me in platitudes.

9. Listen to me, please!

10. Forgive my trespasses, my rudeness and my thoughtlessness.

Suggested Reading

For Caregivers

Braverman, Terry. *When the Going Gets Tough, the Tough Lighten Up!* Los Angeles, Calif.: Mental Floss Publications, 1997.
> Light reading to help keep life in perspective.

Cowman, L. B. *Streams in the Desert.* Grand Rapids, Mich.: Zondervan, 1997.
> A daily devotional especially for people going through difficult times. Good for caregivers to quote from or give as a gift.

Deits, Bob. *Life after Loss.* Tucson, Ariz.: Fisher Books, 1988.
> Practical steps to take for working through the grief process.

Editors of *Prevention* Magazine. *The Doctor's Book of Home Remedies.* Emmaus, Penn.: Rodale Press, 1990.
> Contains hundreds of home remedies that can give comfort easily and inexpensively.

Fitzgerald, Helen. *The Mourning Handbook.* New York: Simon and Schuster, 1994.
> Thorough explanation of grief with good suggestions for caregivers.

Gordon, Arthur. *A Touch of Wonder.* Old Tappan, NJ: Fleming H. Revell, 1974.
> An inspirational, uplifting book for relaxation and pleasure.

Graham, Billy. *Facing Death and Life After.* Waco, Tex.: Word Books, 1987.
> Insightful explanations of life and death issues.

Graham, Laurie. *Rebuilding the House.* New York: Viking Press, 1990.
> A widow writes about her personal experience.

Hurnard, Hannah. *Hind's Feet on High Places.* Wheaton, Ill.: Living Books, 1986.
> A delightful analogy that is an inspiration for anyone going through a difficult time of life; good uplifting reading.

Keating, Kathleen. *Hug Therapy.* New York: MJF Books, 1995.
> A delightful little book for smiles and pleasure.

Kolf, June Cerza. *When Will I Stop Hurting?* Grand Rapids, Mich.: Baker Book House, 1987.
> Information to help grievers in the very early days following a death.

Linn, Erin. *I Know Just How You Feel . . . Avoiding the Clichés of Grief.*
　　Carey, Ill.: Publishers Mark, 1986.
　　　　Extensive information on clichés and the damage they can
　　　　do to grievers.

Lord, Janice Harris. *Beyond Sympathy: What to Say and Do for Someone*
　　Suffering an Injury, Illness or Loss. Ventura, Calif.: Pathfinder Pub.,
　　1988.
　　　　Detailed instructions on ways to help people who are suffering.

McNeill, Donald P., Douglas A. Morrison, and Henri J. M. Nouwen.
　　Compassion: A Reflection on Christian Life. Garden City, New York:
　　Doubleday, 1982.
　　　　Deep, insightful information on serious life issues.

Moody, Raymond A., Jr., M.D. *Life after Life.* New York: Bantam
　　Books, 1988.
　　　　Case histories of people who have been clinically dead
　　　　and survived to tell about their near death experiences.
　　　　Encouraging and informational.

O'Connor, Nancy, Ph.D. *Letting Go with Love.* Tucson, Ariz.:
　　La Mariposa Press, 1994.
　　　　Thorough explanation of the grief process.
　　　　Some good advice for caregivers also.

Veninga, Robert. *A Gift of Hope: How We Survive Our Tragedies.* Boston:
　　Little, Brown, 1985.
　　　　Compiled from hundreds of interviews with people who have
　　　　survived great tragedies. Insightful and encouraging.

Worden, J. William, Ph.D. *Grief Counseling and Grief Therapy: A*
　　Handbook for the Mental Health Practitioner. New York: Springer
　　Publishing Co., 1991.
　　　　A book of technical information written for counselors.
　　　　Valuable information for anyone who wishes to help
　　　　people who are grieving.

For Children

Grollman, Earl. *Explaining Death to Children.* Boston: Beacon Press,
　　1965.
　　　　An easy-to-read, well-written book to help understand
　　　　how grief affects children.

Huntly, Theresa. *Helping Children Grieve*. Minneapolis: Augsburg Press, 1991.
> To help the reader answer children's questions and guide them in coping with their feelings.

Mellonie, Bryan and Robert Ingpen. *Lifetimes: A Beautiful Way to Explain Death to Children*. New York: Bantam, 1983.
> A colorful storybook to read to young children.

Pellegrino, Marjorie White. *I Don't Have an Uncle Phil Anymore*. Washington, D.C.: Magination Press, 1998.
> Following the unexpected death of his uncle, a boy travels to the funeral with his extended family and begins to think about what the event will mean for all of them.

Schaefer, Dan and Christine Lyons. *How Do We Tell the Children?: A Parent's Guide to Helping Children Understand and Cope when Someone Dies*. New York: Newmarket Press, 1986.
> Everything a person needs to know about dealing with children of all ages and death. Special crisis section for quick reference.

Slattery, Kathryn and David C. Cook. *Grandma I'll Miss You: A Child's Story about Death and New Life*. Elfin, Ill.: Chariot Books, 1993.
> A good way to introduce children to death before their lives are touched by it.

Viorst, Judith. *The Tenth Good Thing About Barney*. New York: Atheneum, 1971.
> In an attempt to overcome his grief, a boy tries to think of the ten best things about his dead cat.

Helpful Organizations

In Case of Suicide Threats

Check your local telephone book for suicide prevention phone numbers. Or contact

United States

National Mental Health
  Association
1021 Prince Street
Alexandria, VA 22314
Tel: (703) 684-7722

Website: http://www.nmha.org

Suicide prevention hotline:
  (800) 444-9999

Canada

Suicide Information and Education Centre in Calgary—Includes helpful lists of suicide prevention services in all the Canadian provinces.

Website: http://www.siec.ca

For Cancer Information

United States

American Cancer Society, Inc.
90 Park Avenue
New York, NY 10016
Tel: (212) 736-3030

Website: http://www.cancer.org

Cancer Care, Inc.
1180 Avenue of the Americas
New York, NY 10036
Tel: (212) 221-3300
(800) 813-HOPE

Website:
http://www.cancercare.org

Canada

Canadian Cancer Society and
  National Cancer Institute
  of Canada
10 Alcorn Avenue, Suite 200
Toronto, Ontario M4V 3B1
Tel: (416) 961-7223
Fax: (416) 961-4189

Website: http://www.cancer.ca

For Widowed Persons

United States

Widowed Persons Service
AARP
1909 K Street N.W.
Washington, DC 20049
Tel: (800) 424-3410

Website:
http://www.aarp.org/grief
  program/

Canada

Widowed Support Group of
  Ottawa-Carlton
PO Box 16087, Station F
Ottawa, ON K2C 3S9, Canada
Tel: (613) 723-0010

On Line

Canadian Association of
  Retired Persons

Website: http://www.fifty-plus.net

WidowNet

Website: http://www.fortnet.com/
  WidowNet

For Grieving Parents

United States

The Compassionate Friends
PO Box 3696
Oak Brook, IL 60522
Tel: (630) 990-0010

Website:
http://www.compassionate
  friends.org

National SIDS Alliance
1314 Bedford Avenue, Suite 210
Baltimore, MD 21208
Tel: (800) 221-SIDS
Fax: (410) 964-8009

Website:
http://www.sidsalliance.org

Parents of Murdered Children
100 E. 8th Street B-41
Cincinnati, OH 45202
Tel: (513) 721-5083

Website: http://www.pomc.com

Canada

The Compassionate Friends of
  Canada National Office
685 William Avenue
Winnepeg, Manitoba R3E 0Z2
Tel: (204) 787-2460

Families and Friends of Victims of Violent Death

United States

Families of Homicide Victims
  Victim Services
2 LaFayette Street
New York, NY 10007
Tel: (212) 577-7700
Fax: (212) 385-0331

Mothers Against Drunk Driving
  (MADD)
669 Airport Freeway, Suite 310
Hurst, TX 76053
Hotline: 1-800-438-MADD

Website: http://www.MADD.org

Families and Friends of Suicide Victims

United States

Seasons: Suicide Bereavement, Inc.
4777 Maniloa Drive
Salt Lake City, UT 84117
Tel: (801) 649-8327

Survivors of Suicide (SOS)
St. Joseph's Hospital
5000 W. Chambers Street
Milwaukee, WI 53210

Canada

Canadian Mental Health
  Association
Suicide Services
Tel: (403) 297-1744 (9-5 P.M.)
(403) 266-1605 after hours

Community Lifelines
138 Kerr Drive
Sault Ste. Marie
Ontario P6A 5H9

Website:
http://www3.sympatico.ca

On Line

PBS and Weblab on Suicide
  Survivors
Website:
http://www.pbs.org/weblab/
  living

For suicide survivors
http://www.1000deaths.com

Grief Support for Children

United States

The Good Grief Program at
  Boston Medical Center
1 Boston Medical Place MAT 5
Boston, MA 02118
Tel: (617) 414-4005
Fax: (617) 414-7219
e-mail: mtrozzi@bu.edu

The Dougy Center
The National Center for Grieving
  Children and Families
PO Box 86852
Portland, OR 97286

Website: http://www.dougy.org

Grief Support for Teenagers

United States

Teen Age Grief, Inc. (TAG)
PO Box 22034
Newhall, CA 91322
Tel: (805) 253-1932

General Information

United States

American Psychiatric Association
1400 K Street NW
Washington, DC 20005
Tel: (202) 682-6000

Website: http://www.psych.org

American Psychological
  Association
750 First Street NE
Washington, DC 20002
Tel: (202) 336-5500

Website: http://www.apa.org

National Association of
  Social Workers
750 First Street, Suite 700
Washington, DC 20002
Tel: (202) 408-8600
Fax: (202) 336-8331

Website:
http://www.socialworkers.org

Canada

Bereavement Services Canada
Tel: (905) 628-6008

Maggie's Place
129 Arthur Place
Truro, Nova Scotia B2N 1Y2
Tel: (902) 893-4321, Ext. 140

On Line Grief Support

United States

Grief Recovery On Line
Website: http://www.groww.com

Canada

Centre for the Grief Journey
Website:
http://www.grieftalk.com

Index